Lisa

Believe!

Dream!

God loves you
and so do I! :)

Jy A. Paz

MW01595084

Loretta Williams

Ben Deus
719 6609246

Loretta
719 439 3909

The Agony and Ecstasy
of the Bipolar Mind

Old and New Healing Methods that give
Hope to All Humanity

JOY A. PAZ

WestBow
PRESS
A DIVISION OF THOMAS NELSON

Copyright © 2013 Joy A. Paz.

All rights reserved. No part of this book may be used or reproduced by any means,
graphic, electronic, or mechanical, including photocopying, recording, taping or by any
information storage retrieval system without the written permission of the publisher
except in the case of brief quotations embodied in critical articles and reviews.

All names and institutions have been changed to protect the innocent.

Biblical references are from the New International Version, 1984,
New American Standard Version, 1995, New King James Version, 1980.

Music and lyrics for "It Is No Secret" are by Stuart Hamblen (1950).

Music and lyrics for "I Am a Promise" by Bill and Gloria Gaither

WestBow Press books may be ordered through booksellers or by contacting:

WestBow Press
A Division of Thomas Nelson
1663 Liberty Drive
Bloomington, IN 47403
www.westbowpress.com
1-(866) 928-1240

Because of the dynamic nature of the Internet, any web addresses or links contained in
this book may have changed since publication and may no longer be valid. The views
expressed in this work are solely those of the author and do not necessarily reflect the
views of the publisher, and the publisher hereby disclaims any responsibility for them.

Certain stock imagery © Thinkstock.
Any people depicted in stock imagery provided by Thinkstock are models,
and such images are being used for illustrative purposes only.

ISBN: 978-1-4497-9007-3 (sc)
ISBN: 978-1-4497-9009-7 (hc)
ISBN: 978-1-4497-9008-0 (e)

Library of Congress Control Number: 2013905854

Printed in the United States of America.

WestBow Press rev. date: 4/4/2013

Contents

This book is dedicated to my children, Mary and David, who have so enriched my life and who have been a tremendous blessing from God. They have made a great success of their lives and have honored their father and me. I wish them all the success in achieving all their goals, dreams, and aspirations. My prayer is that they continue to use their potential and possibilities to glorify their Creator; to show love to all the people they encounter through life; and to inspire others to pursue excellence in their lives, using all the talents, gifts, and potential that they also have received from God.

Foreword

With highest esteem, I applaud Joy Paz for her accomplishment in compiling a work that gives such insightful understanding of the world of those whose lives have been affected by bipolar disorder and its influences, both the victims and those in the victims' environment. Having known of Joy's faithful course of life for over thirty years, I am not surprised that she has chosen to share insight into what she has extensively researched and personally experienced in order to help make the lives of those who read this book a little better,...a little richer,...and a little less desolate.

I have had the privilege of working with Joy in the setting of Christian Children's Homes in several states; the last one being Wilson Children's Home in Memphis. I have found her to be staunchly consistent in her desire to serve God unwaveringly as she serves her family, her friends, and her fellow man. She is a tireless advocate for the suffering, a compassionate friend to the lonely and hurting, and a constant source of strength for the fallen and cast down.

As you enter into the pages of this book, I assure you that you are reading the heart of a Proverbs 31 woman, for Joy certainly exemplifies all the qualities of a virtuous woman. Read her with passion. Expect a blessing. You will not be disappointed.

Dewayne Barton, MS
Executive Director of Wilson Children's Home

Preface

 verybody has a story to tell. This book is largely a memoir about John and me, but it also includes information about treatments, old and new healing methods for everyone, a timeline of events in the appendix, a glossary, and resources. I have researched extensively through books and webinars on the Internet by world-renowned speakers for knowledge and understanding. Every human being is so precious to the Creator, and everybody affects the world for good or bad. However, not everybody has touched as many lives for good from so many different countries as my husband, John Paz, has in his lifetime. This is in spite of the fact that he had bipolar disorder, a form of mental disorder, which manifested itself when he was fifty-seven years old. I believe our story will encourage others in their walk in this life. I have been touched by many bipolar authors who have written of their experiences in so many facets of life. It is the goal of this writing to encourage those people who dare to dream big dreams and to educate others who are struggling with mental illnesses, especially bipolar disorder. It is a rare thing when both a husband and wife suffer from this same mental disorder. This happened to us, twenty-three years apart—we both "lost our marbles" (meaning we both had a mental breakdown as adults). In 1950, when I was five years old, I lost my big cat-eye marble. It was my greatest possession in life. Well, some godly Bible teacher taught me that we should ask God for help when we are in trouble, and I was in trouble. I can still remember asking God to help me find my cat-eye marble. Then I searched high and low around the dining room table and sure enough, I found my marble! God has been my friend ever since. Thirty years later, I really "lost my marbles" and succumbed to this troubling bipolar disorder. God restored my most precious possession: my mind. In this writing, I will reveal that both my husband, John, and I "lost our marbles" and that God guided and sustained us on our journey in life.

I was thirty-five when I succumbed to the manic phase of bipolar disorder. I have seen many people suffer for years, along with their families, because they have this disorder, but doctors did not diagnose them properly. People must realize they need to see a psychiatrist who is an expert in treating this disorder.

Dr. Ronald Fieve, a psychiatrist who specializes in the treatment of mood disorders, wrote the book *Moodswing*, in which he discusses bipolar disorder in detail. Dr. Fieve notes that many highly successful and creative people have had this illness. He also describes in great detail the moods of great men such as Abraham Lincoln, Theodore Roosevelt, Winston Churchill, and others. I feel an obligation to share the experiences we have had in the hope of educating and encouraging susceptible individuals, giving them hope so that their family's suffering can be minimized. It is my intention to whet the appetite with this book and spur mankind on to the potential of every human being. I believe God can take a wretched life and transform that life into a beautiful human being, even when one has bipolar disorder and no matter what has happened previously in life. In the end, it is as the song goes: "It is no secret what God can do. What He's done for others, He'll do for you."

Acknowledgments

I first want to acknowledge God, my Creator, who gave me the abundant life and instilled within me talents and abilities and the joy of using these gifts to glorify Him.

I acknowledge my husband, John, who inspired the writing of this book. We shared thirty-six blessed years "dancing" on three continents and sharing the Gospel to the country of Brazil for eight years.

I acknowledge my parents and John's parents for their unconditional love for us and for a home filled with laughter, love, and great examples of Christian character.

I acknowledge the Brazil mission teams consisting of hundreds of the most dedicated, spiritually minded, love-driven human beings who touched my heart and inspired me, while working in Brazil, to "soar on the wings of eagles"; where I did "run and not grow weary"; where I walked and did not faint (Isaiah 40:31, NIV).

With so much gratitude and appreciation, I acknowledge WestBow Press for the incredible care they gave my book and the manner in which they treated me with professionalism and genuine concern. The editors were extraordinary in their knowledge and expertise.

They made sense of my scatterbrained writing. I look forward to the publishing of "our" book and believe it will be a success because of God, WestBow, and all the people who have touched my heart in this exciting and adventurous life that I have experienced.

I acknowledge Dr. Angelo D. Christian, the most compassionate and brilliant geriatric neuropsychiatrist, who touched John's and my life. He showed an enormous amount of patience and perseverance, not only with John but also with all his patients of all ages.

Chapter 1
Bipolar Adventures

My father succumbed to bipolar disorder in his twenties. After about a year, he recovered by taking a crude form of shock treatments, such as putting him in a hot shower and quickly turning it very cold. This was around 1930, before electric shock treatments became available. In the 1930s, not much was understood about mental illness, so for ten months, my father was chained to the floor in an asylum. He was also beaten at times. He recovered and went on to have a full and rewarding life. He was stable for the rest of his life, without medicine or psychiatrists. When he was much older, he served as a leader of the church, both in Ohio and Florida. He lived a full life and died at the age of 91.

One of the aspects of bipolar disorder is impulsiveness. For example, when my father was twenty-seven and my mother was twenty-one, they met in Florida on a Friday and married on the next Monday. Their total courtship lasted three days, yet they were married for sixty-four years! They were both from Ohio, living about forty miles from each other, but never met there. My mother was engaged to a man at the time she met my dad, and they had already bought their furniture. Imagine the look on his face when he found out his fiancée was married to another man! I do not recommend this at all but mention it merely to illustrate the extreme impulsivity of bipolar disorder. In my case, impulsiveness from my bipolar disorder showed up when I was five years old. I wanted to fly. One day, my father was driving fast on a dirt road, and I turned to my older brother, Jake, and told him I was going to open the car door to see if I could fly. I don't remember if I flew, because I was knocked unconscious when I hit the ground. The doctor later had to remove stones that had been ground into my head, giving a new meaning to the phrase "you have rocks in your head."

Jake and I fought a lot. He was jealous of me for getting so much attention from our parents, as I was the baby of the family and the only daughter. My oldest brother was a Down syndrome child who was put in an institution at six years old so that my parents could better raise Jake and me. He died at the age of sixty-two, which is much older than most Down syndrome children's life expectancy. He never spoke a word in his life. He could cry, laugh, and make noises, but the doctor said that his brain just did not develop to be able to speak.

Mental illness can be hereditary. My mother always said I was just like my father. He never wanted to talk about his mental breakdown, as it was such a painful experience. My mother explained to me as much as she knew about his mental breakdown—that he was trying to do too much during his sophomore year in college. He was on the track team, which traveled a lot to track meets, as well as dating, which also took up a lot of time. This, in addition to his schoolwork, caused enormous stress in his life. Extreme stress can trigger bipolar disorder.

When I was a sophomore in college, I was taking several classes and dating John. In my sophomore literature class, I studied Plato, Socrates, and other deep thinkers that required strong focus on this reading. I was in love and could not concentrate on Greek scholars; my thoughts were on John, not Plato. I did not want to be like my father by doing too much and having a breakdown, so I dropped that course, even though I had a B in the course at that point. I was afraid that I, too, could have a mental breakdown.

My father went into the manic phase that went into a psychosis. I had the same manifestation as he did, as this is part of the manic state of bipolar disorder. We both had an intense energy for great and glorious accomplishments. The thought that I was just like him had been planted in the recesses of my mind. I believed it—and it was true; I inherited that bipolar gene.

God can perform wonders through people who have bipolar disorder. The apostle Paul stated, "For when I am weak, then I am strong" (2 Corinthians 12:10, NIV). John and I had an incredible drive that produced an amazing amount of energy to accomplish many projects on three continents. Many actors, actresses, poets, and authors are or have been bipolar.

A positive aspect of bipolar disorder is the abundant creativity, inspiration, and drive that flowed from my brain when I was in the manic state—I was in ecstasy and required little sleep. From the age of thirty to thirty-five, I lived in the mental state of hypomania, which is a mild high but within reality. John, unfortunately, possessed the agony side of bipolar disorder and suffered pain, torment, and the abyss of despair. One psychiatrist informed me, however, that John was in hypomania most of his life, until he had his breakdown at the age of fifty-seven; then severe depression took over.

I remember my parents played a certain record when I was a very little girl. One of the songs repeated, "It is no secret what God can do. What He's done for others, He'll do for you." I believe this message influenced me throughout my life. This is the theme song for this book, because even though one has bipolar disorder, with God's help, there is the possibility of great accomplishments and a rewarding life.

Chapter 2
The Early Years

here is a Scripture that says, "Now to Him who is able to do immeasurably more than all we *ask* or *imagine*, according to His *power* that is at work within us, to *Him* be the *glory* in the church and in Christ Jesus throughout all *generations, forever and ever*" (Ephesians 3:20, NIV [emphasis mine]). This is John's and my story of all that God accomplished in our lives—more than I could have dreamed possible—yet lurking deep within us was a predisposition for bipolar disorder.

John Paz was born at home in Greenbrier, West Virginia, on July 10, 1946. He was raised on a farm with old-fashioned values, where it was his duty to milk cows before daylight, as well as other chores. John attended a two-room schoolhouse. This is significant, as he now holds the degree of Doctor of Ministry, in spite of his humble beginnings and a poor early education. He learned a good work ethic early in life, along with other Christian values, from his remarkable parents, Floyd and Alberta Paz. I have such love and admiration for them to this day. His mother was one of the most intelligent, innovative, wise, and loving people I have ever known. John's father had only an eighth-grade education but owned and operated three businesses. He was a giant of a man in character. I pay tribute to both of them.

John attended Barker Christian University in Memphis. While there, he preached on Sunday mornings at a country church outside Little Rock, Arkansas. Traveling to and from church every Sunday—a three-hour drive—greatly limited his study time, but it seemed to me that he always was able to accomplish most any task much faster than anyone else, whether it was term papers or sermons. He had a strong drive with an enormous amount of energy, which I later learned was characteristic of a bipolar mind, a racing to accomplish great and glorious things. This was the positive side of bipolar disorder. John had a Bible major with a minor in speech.

We worked together in the dining hall at the university, and it seemed to me as if this character could tackle anything. He dated nearly every girl on campus and was loved and respected by everyone. It was during this time at the university that John became known as a compassionate counselor, because so many students with problems knew they could go to him for counseling. Students could see that John had a compassionate and humble nature and that he really cared for them.

While at the university—this was in the 1960s—I broke two of their rules. I am not proud of that, and it's a good thing I wasn't caught, as I probably would have been expelled. I just believed these rules were too strict. One rule was that when male preacher students went on their trips to preach, they could not bring their girlfriends with them. Well, John and another preacher student would go together, to take turns preaching on Sunday mornings and Sunday nights. Once in a while my friend, who was dating this other fellow, and I would ride to Little Rock with them. We didn't do anything wrong on these trips, but the college administrators believed it would tempt students to engage in immoral conduct. I was taking a chance on this behavior, as it took several hours to go to and return from this little church in the country.

The other rule was that female residents could not ride in a car with a boy to go to the Christian camp, which was located just a few miles from the campus. The camp was used for retreats and summer camps. One day in January, John asked me to go with him to the camp. (He broke these rules too!) We went to what is called "B rock," the highest point of the camp with a breathtaking view of the foothills of the Ozarks. It was there and then that John proposed to me. As we were sitting on the "top of the world," I said yes, and about that time we heard gunshots. Somebody apparently was hunting and didn't know we were up there, and we didn't know anyone was around. We hit the ground on our backs, fearing we would be shot. (I sure didn't want to have a shotgun wedding!) I made it back to my dorm, and my roommates were somewhat surprised to see that I had wet leaves all over my back. They knew that John proposed to me, but I don't think they believed me when I told them what really happened. Fortunately, I was not caught by the college officials, but I have great memories of John proposing to me and the fear of being shot to death after saying yes to his proposal!

While at Barker Christian University, I dreamed of going into mission work. I pictured myself in the jungles of Africa, telling people about the great God that I knew; telling them that He had sent His only Son to save humanity. So many Africans had never heard the name of Jesus. What a challenge! I had a strong drive with a purpose to accomplish my dreams.

At the same time that I was dreaming about Africa, John was dreaming of doing mission work one day in Thailand. We were continents apart in our dreams...but God had a plan.

We married in 1967, and John finished his bachelor's degree in 1968. We decided to work with another race of people in Memphis, Tennessee, before going to the mission field; this was to help us acclimate to another culture. In 1969, we became house parents for a county agency to thirteen African American teenage girls from the worst homes in that area. I was the only white person to attend my girls' PTA meetings. We learned a lot about this culture.

I really grew to love those girls. One weekend several of them were gone on visits to relatives, so only five were at home with me. We decided to go get a hamburger. This was in an all-black part of town. While at the fast-food place, a man drew a knife on another man, and I had to quickly get my girls back to the car. More and more people gathered around. The police came with their dogs, and soon there was a riot. We got out of that situation safely, but sitting in that locked car with my girls while the riot was going on was quite frightening—we had to wait, as it was impossible to leave that area because my car was blocked by police cars and a crowd of onlookers.

I often had to manhandle the girls, as they became enraged easily. They would lash out at me by kicking me in the stomach or trying to hit me whenever any little thing didn't go their way. They had been abused and neglected most of their lives and had so much hostility bottled up. One day, while John was at work, I took the girls' snack away from them as a disciplinary measure for not obeying me. I had to lock myself in John's and my private quarters in the home, as the girls threw every book in their library at my door. I had to call the sheriff, as the girls were having their own riot. I was pregnant with our daughter at this time, so John and I decided it was time to move on. John completed his master's degree at the Barker Graduate School of Religion in Memphis, Tennessee.

Chapter 3
Brazil's Jungle, Joys, and Challenges

When our daughter was a year old in 1971, we were on our way—not to Africa or Thailand but to Brazil! We discovered that God's plan for us wasn't the African continent or the Asian continent but the South American continent—and we had to learn to speak Portuguese, the Brazilian language.

It was on the foreign mission field that I truly became aware of the amazing character of the man I married. I saw the beauty of God shining in him; all the glory should go to our Creator, who made this incredible man! When our daughter, Mary, was a toddler and I was expecting our son, David, John constantly took trips to the Brazilian interior. He would fly in the single-engine private plane owned by the missionaries, just him and the pilot, in an area where the cows had to be cleared from the runway before they could land.

The "interior of Brazil" refers to a more backward civilization, such as mud huts and thatched roofs. I often lay awake at night, wondering if John would come back alive from those trips. Thousands of Brazilians in the interior were completing Bible correspondence courses offered by the missionaries, and many Brazilians wanted someone to come to study the Bible with them. One trip involved a couple who were very poor and illiterate, and the husband had leprosy. One of his hands had rotted off. His wife had only one good dress, and she was washing it the day John and the pilot went to visit them. She was unable to fix them coffee because she didn't have anything proper to wear—John saw her dress drying on the line. The husband explained to John that he had prayed for the Lord to protect him and his wife, so that when these men came to teach them the Bible, they would tell the truth.

One day in Sao Paulo where we lived, which at the time was the third-largest city in the world, I saw a man with leprosy. His hand was rotting off, and it upset me for the rest of the day. I did not have the courage to get near him. John, however, went back to the interior and taught this man with leprosy and his wife that God loved them and sent His only Son to die for their sins too. This is another indication of the Christian quality of compassion that John had in his heart.

John told many stories about the deprived interior. One couple, recently married, told John they never had a picture taken together. This brought out John's sensitivity, because he understood how much it would mean to them to have a picture of themselves as newlyweds. John took their picture and had it developed. Then, the next time he flew to the interior, he gave the photograph to them. There was so much rejoicing over one simple picture. Friends and relatives were so happy for this simple pleasure in life. Who among us would ever think we would be married without a picture of that glorious day? This was in the early 1970s; much has changed since then. Another story of John's compassion and sensitivity was when a poor crippled lady needed a wheelchair to go to church. John was able to see that she got a wheelchair so she could go to worship.

Portuguese is a beautiful language, but it did not come easily for John; it was a great struggle. It was easier for me. They say that women hear the rhythm of a language better, and it's easier for women to learn it. (I like to talk, so I had to learn how to communicate!) In spite of that obstacle, the love of God came through in John's actions, and the Brazilians responded to his caring and compassionate nature. They had to chuckle many times when, for example, John was preaching, and he used the word *galo*, meaning rooster, when he thought he'd said "tree branches" (*galho*). The two words are very close in pronunciation. Then there was the time when a new missionary friend preached an entire sermon on "God's glasses." He thought he was saying "the oracles of God," but he said the *oculos* (glasses) of God. The words are so similar. Another time, one of the men in our group—a very proper person—was in a department store. He was just studying the language, but he needed to find a restroom, so he went up to a young lady and thought he asked for the men's bathroom. What he actually asked her, however, was "Where is the men's pine tree?" Pine tree in Portuguese is *pinheiro*, and bathroom is *banheiro*.

I have made some crazy mistakes in the language also. One time I thought I was saying I wanted to buy a coconut cake, but I put the accent on the wrong part of the word. What I actually said was that I wanted some "shit" cake. At the time, I wondered why the clerk kept repeating that word back to me. After that, I changed my flavor to pineapple!

In 1970 land had been cleared from the jungle area in the state of Sao Paulo to construct a camp for young people. John was the assistant director at the camp in 1971 and 1972. We loved working with the young people. One of the young men with whom John worked at the camp went on to become an engineer and, thirty years later, the president of the board of directors of the children's home in Brazil.

At the camp, we encountered vampire bats, which sucked the blood of our horses; some very dangerous snakes; and colorful tropical birds and animals. One day as I walked along a trail by myself, a six-foot green iguana, which had ridges like a dinosaur, ran right out in front of me. That was the last time I walked alone in the jungle. However, there was a native Brazilian man of Indian descent who had a profound knowledge of jungle life. He took a few of us through the thick of the jungle, where huge plants wrapped all around the trees. Droplets of water on the huge tropical leaves and thick forestation sparkled in the sun. He explained which plants could be used to give water, like a type of lily that could be turned upside down and water would come out. He also showed us which plants could be made into rope. It was truly fascinating.

I was told wild jaguars lived there but fortunately, we did not encounter any. This thick forestation gives off incredible amounts of rich oxygen. There used to be monkeys at the campsite, but they went deeper into the jungle when the area was cleared for the camp. Black panthers were still in this area.

We hung Coke bottles in the open barn where the horses stayed at night. Somehow, the Coke bottles scared the vampire bats and kept them away from the horses. One dark night, as we were in our cabin, John really wanted a cup of coffee. The coffee was in the main building, which was close by, but I can't believe I ventured forth from our cabin and walked alone at night—knowing there were dangerous snakes, vampire bats, huge iguanas, deadly insects, black panthers, and all types of scary creatures—to get my man a cup of coffee. (That is called *love* … or stupidity!)

I now have a better understanding of how the Indians in the Amazon rain forest survive—I learned that the Brazilian jungle has many herbs for all types of infirmities. I used to purchase herbs in the city. One example of an herb that comes from the Amazon rainforest is graviola.

<u>Can graviola cure cancer?</u> Graviola comes from a tree in the rain forest of Africa, South America and Southeast Asia. People in these countries use graviola to treat infections with viruses or parasites, arthritis, depression and other conditions. It has been shown in laboratory studies that graviola extracts can kill some types of liver and breast cancer cells.

This discovery has been challenged by some medical organizations. I am a kidney cancer survivor. If I ever have cancer again, I would definitely search out this plant treatment. My feeling is that someday, the rich, vast plants and trees of the Amazon will provide many cures for diseases that now plague humanity.

Also found in the Amazon jungle is the type of palm tree that produces the acai (pronounced *ah-see-i*) fruit. This type of palm tree cannot grow anywhere else in the world, as it needs the environment of the Amazon jungle. Many other herbs have been discovered in Brazil. While I was in Brazil, I used to get many herbs in their raw state and eat them. If only people would go back to nature's healing herbs and food, many people would not be suffering so from the Western diet of processed food, sugar, preservatives, unhealthy additives, natural foods stripped of their nutrients, fluoride, chlorine, etc.

God protected our family in this potentially dangerous jungle area while we worked with the young people. There were many coral snakes at the camp. One day I saw several girls with our toddler daughter, cornering a coral snake. One has only thirty minutes to live if bitten by a coral snake and not given the shot of the antivenin. I grabbed her and ran away from that area. Another time, John went fishing on the Sucuri River, deep in the interior of Brazil. *Sucuri* is the Portuguese word for the huge anaconda snake, which is bigger than a python. They named the river after the snake, because there were so many in that area. I was very uneasy about John going to that location, but John came back without any sign of anacondas—and also without any fish. "The angel of the Lord encamps around those who fear him, and he delivers them" (Psalm 34:7, NIV).

Our son, David, was born in October 1972. In 1973 John and I, along with three other couples, established a church near the metro area of Sao Paulo. This church was in a strategic location for millions of inhabitants.

One day our family and another American and his Brazilian wife went deep into a forest to have a picnic. After about an hour, we came to a clearing in the forest, where we saw a big, beautiful house. The Brazilian lady said it belonged to a Nazi family. After World War II, many Nazis emigrated to Brazil and Argentina, but it was a bit of a shock to realize a Nazi family lived hidden away in the forest. I was glad we didn't encounter them. How often do you go on a picnic and run into the Nazis?

When we lived in Sao Paulo, our section of the city had people of three big religions. Down the street from us lived Brazilians who were descendents and slaves from Africa. They were called Spiritists. At midnight, on special nights, they would take an animal, usually a cat, and go to the nearest intersection to make a sacrifice and then cut out the heart of the animal. They believed that the evil spirit would then enter the next living thing they saw. They would then kill that animal or bird. We regularly found dead cats near our front yard and other locations. The older missionaries told us not to be around those intersections during those rituals. We heard that in northern Brazil, these people actually killed a person who was around there at that time of sacrificing.

I encountered a depth of evil in Brazil that I never had in the States. One day I met a teenage girl who told me with pride that she blasphemed God! She also said she could read people's minds. What was so scary is that she was just in high school, and no matter what questions I asked her about history, science, and other subjects, she knew as much or more than I did, and I had attended three universities! I felt the evil so strong that I just wanted to run away from her, but then I remembered that the one inside me (Jesus) was stronger than the evil one. After several years of confronting this evil, I grew very weary spiritually, and I sought relief. I felt like I was led to one of the beautiful parks in our city. I sat down by the quiet waters and remembered the Scripture of the Twenty-Third Psalm, verse 2, which says, "He leads me beside quiet waters." (NIV). Then I saw several cages of birds and black doves. To my amazement, I looked up and on top of one of those cages was a pure-white dove with his eye looking straight at me. I was comforted and remembered instances where the dove is spoken about in the Bible, especially at the baptism of Jesus, where the Spirit descended on Jesus in Matthew 3:16. "When He had been baptized, Jesus came up immediately from the water; and behold the heavens were opened to Him, and He saw the *Spirit of God* descending like a *dove* and alighting upon Him." (NIV). After being surrounded by so much evil, the very sight of this pure-white dove showed me that God, through His Spirit, was strengthening me in my inner being. He renewed my soul.

Every morning at six o'clock (seven o'clock on Sundays), I heard a bongo-drum sound down the other side of our street. I thought it was noise from some kind of factory. Early one morning, I walked up to where the noise was and to my amazement, I saw a building with the door open and a gigantic white Buddha inside made of white marble. (Brazil is very rich in marble and semiprecious stones, as well as diamonds and emeralds. Our house had marble in the kitchen and in our bathrooms.) Several Japanese, dressed in all-white clothing, entered this building. They were pounding drums loudly—that was the noise I heard—which I assumed was part of their worship.

All around us were houses with their own personal idol—St. Thomas, St. Jude, or other saints—sitting somewhere on the front porch. The people thought this would protect the family residing there. Everywhere, nations seek the Divine. It hurts to see so many people lost from so many nations due to ignorance. They need to know the great I AM. "Be still and know that I am God" (Psalm 46:10, NIV). God once said that His people were destroyed for lack of knowledge.

We left Sao Paulo, Brazil, in 1974 and spent about a year in the States, where John preached and I taught a ladies Bible class. Occasionally, we hear of people who insist they had an out-of-body experience. I believe I experienced that at the age of thirty. It was early in 1975. I had a dream so real that it seemed to transcend time and space. It wasn't just a dream; it was a spiritual state of being. In the dream, I heard a voice that I perceived as the Spirit say to me that I needed to see myself as I really was. I moaned and said no one wants to see herself as she really is. He insisted, however, and when I saw myself as I really was—with all of my shortcomings—I was very sorrowful, and I cried. Then the Spirit carried me to a gold-studded mountain and told me to climb that shiny, slippery mountain. When I said it was humanly impossible to climb it, He showed me a small, narrow pathway up that mountain, and He said, "With God's help, you can climb that mountain."

I suddenly woke up, gasping for air, as if I had not been breathing for some time. It was really like an out-of-body experience. Even though this was many years ago, I remember it like it was yesterday. So truly, God has been helping me climb my many mountains.

Not long ago, I shared this dream with John, as I believed he needed to see himself as he really was, with all his negative, trapped emotions. Then he could be set free from the agony that he had suffered for so many years, but it would mean that he would need to face a tremendous amount of pain.

In the fall of 1975, John and I and three other couples moved to Campinas, Brazil. We did not realize that this city was the homosexual capital of Brazil! We established the church after a lot of struggle and by overcoming many obstacles. We worked as a team, and God blessed the work. Today, there are three thriving churches in this city, which is now known as the most violent city in Brazil—what a challenge!

It was during the four and a half years of our stay in Campinas that John and another missionary started making plans to start a children's home in Brazil. The need was phenomenal. There were so many street children—hungry and needy orphans.   M a n y years ago, the street children in Rio de Janeiro were such a nuisance that the police would line up children and shoot them to death. They didn't have a Department of Human Services to deal with these children. The word got out to Europe and the United States that Brazil was doing this, so they had to stop that shocking behavior. This happened many years before we were there, but the need for Christian children's homes was still urgent. Brazil depended on tourism from all over the world to visit the incredibly beautiful city of Rio de Janeiro. I have visited Rio de Janeiro four times, and it is a very dangerous place. One day we were driving in a van, and there was a van next to us that was full of policemen or military men with their machine guns out the window, probably chasing a drug cartel, as that was a big problem there.

One of John's biggest projects was the *LAR Cristao de Assistencia a Menores* (Christian Home of Assistance to Minors) in Rio de Janeiro, or "the LAR," as we called it. John's dream in 1975 of starting a children's home happened in God's own time. John and another missionary made plans for the home, all the architectural and governmental documentation was completed, and a Brazilian Christian lawyer and others were on the board. The LAR was operated by an American widow who lived forty-two years in Brazil as a missionary. She and her husband started this children's home in Rio. This lady's health was deteriorating, so she returned to the States. The conditions were not good at all in Rio for the children. There were drug dealers and other violent people surrounding the LAR. A missionary's Brazilian wife, Neusa, had inherited a big hacienda and a lot of land in the state of Sao Paulo. She donated some of the land for the children's home. Because of her generosity, the Brazilian home was able to move to the state of Sao Paulo. Twenty-three years later, this home would be sponsored by a children's home in Memphis, where John would become the executive director.

When we lived in Campinas, Brazil, I jogged in the jungle at least five days a week. The huge jungle area was left intact on the outside of the city, so I would drive our children to school and then on the way back, I would jog and breathe in all the rich oxygen. There were lions, a monkey island, and many other animals in this area, like a mini-zoo. Also, I would pass a chocolate tree. One time I ran in the rain, and it was so glorious—I got an emotional high from that experience. Brazil is a lush, beautiful country.

In 1977, I almost died in Brazil due to unknowingly eating some rotten codfish. I knew I was close to death, but John noticed that at that moment, I seemed to radiate with a glow. I was so listless and weak that when I went to the hospital, I was severely dehydrated. The doctor said I was strong, or I would not have made it. As I sat in his office, dying, he looked at me and said in an English accent, "You have a Hollywood way about you." I guess he saw my radiance too, but I was thankful to be alive.

Chapter 4
Altered States of Consciousness

The mind is capable of many things. In 1979, I suffered a pseudo-pregnancy. A doctor in Brazil examined me and said I was six weeks pregnant, with the threat of miscarriage. I wasn't pregnant at all, but I believed that I was. My mind so influenced my body that I even fooled the doctor. Eventually, a compassionate doctor sat down with me and explained that I had just made up this pregnancy in my mind. John had had a vasectomy years before this, but I just reasoned that his tubes had grown back together. Do you see the madness here?

I worked hard in missionary work, which I loved, but in January, February, and March 1979, I experienced the blackness of depression. There was no logical reason for the depression. I had a beautiful new house in Brazil, a wonderful husband and two adorable children, and was achieving all my dreams and goals beyond my wildest expectations. Therefore, I should not have been depressed. The depression was like a cloud over me, like a burden I couldn't shake. This cloud of depression, however, just lifted after three months, without my taking any medication or seeing a doctor. It never returned.

This was a challenging experience. I learned later that it was a chemical imbalance in my brain. We had just returned from the

United States where we were on furlough for three months, traveling to several states and visiting supporting churches and relatives. Our brand new Brazilian house was constructed by a man who built it for his wife, but she decided it was too big. The house cost only about thirty-five thousand dollars in our money, but it was equivalent to several hundred thousand dollars in the States. It had a beautiful living room with wall-to-wall carpeting, which was very rare at that time in Brazil. The house had a sunken dining room, with a winter garden outside the double glass doors. I had all kinds of beautiful tropical plants, a Belgium canary, and two lovely parakeets in this glorious garden. Beautiful Brazilian wood was throughout the house. Our two big bathrooms had marble as well as colorful tile all the way to the ceiling. There were bidets in each bathroom like the French have. There was a maid's quarters in the back of our property that had a room and bathroom, where a sweet, single, legally blind lady lived with us for two years. She accomplished so many aspects of normal living, even though she could see only shadows. She was born with syphilis, having contracted the disease from her mother, which caused her blindness. She used all her other senses as well as intuition and taught me much about the incredible power and abilities of handicapped people. However, one day she was cleaning lettuce when my daughter, who was next to her, screamed at her—a tarantula was hiding in the lettuce, but this woman couldn't see it.

In June 1980, an American missionary family of six came from a small town in Brazil, where they did mission work for several years, and stayed with us for two weeks before they returned to the States permanently. One week during their stay with us, I had to prepare three different children's Bible classes, as we were working with two small congregations in one town and one small group in a nearby city. We had to make all of our own teaching materials, as these were not available in Brazil at this time. That same week I also had to prepare one adult women's Bible class for the American missionary women and one in Portuguese for the Brazilian ladies of the church. I had to translate all the material from English to Portuguese. I suffered a mental overload and crashed, succumbing to the hereditary mental illness. I "lost my marbles," meaning that I went into the manic phase of bipolar disorder. I went on a high that developed into a psychosis due to the extreme stress I was encountering. The stress was too much for me, especially as I had a genetic predisposition for this disorder.

One afternoon I left the house to get my hair fixed, along with a pedicure and manicure—and I wore a beautiful brocade evening gown. Another characteristic of the manic phase is spending money irresponsibly. For a long time I wanted a pair of diamond earrings and a diamond necklace, even though for thirty-six years of our marriage, John had given me jewelry of emeralds, diamonds, rubies, and most of the semiprecious stones. Fortunately, I decided to have lunch before I went on my shopping spree for those diamond earrings and necklace. I went to a restaurant for lunch and was eating when I heard what I thought was God's spiritual voice in my head, asking me if I wanted to go home. (Hearing voices is a sign of psychosis, and I knew that.) I said a silent yes. I first thought He meant going home to Ohio, where my youngest brother was getting married. I really wanted to be at his big wedding. Then I thought He really meant going home to heaven. He asked me how I would like to go, and I said, "If it's all the same to you, God, I would like to go like Elijah did, in a chariot of fire to heaven. "As they were walking along and talking together, suddenly a chariot of fire and horses of fire appeared and separated the two of them, and Elijah went up to heaven in a whirlwind" (2 Kings 2:11, NIV). I always aim high in life! I left the restaurant and started walking in a catatonic state. There was a big cliff ahead, but I saw an arrow pointing to go to the left. In such a catatonic state, bipolar manic persons could easily kill themselves unintentionally, and the public would just assume it was suicide. I then fell into a big ditch. It took several men to get me out because I had an incredible amount of strength—my adrenaline was surging as I waited for my chariot to come for me. I was clearly in a psychotic state. I was taken to a hospital by ambulance, but I figured I was going to heaven from that vehicle instead of a chariot. *What a bummer!* I thought. *I was really looking forward to the chariot ride.*

I love Brazil, but the Brazilian doctors and nurses had no clue about mental illness. The tried to get me to talk, but I refused. One nurse said, "Hit her." One doctor was very compassionate, but another one pinched my nose closed and closed my mouth, so that I couldn't breathe, but I still refused to talk. I commanded my whole body to shut down and conserve oxygen, but then, when I was about to go unconscious, I snapped at him with my teeth, and he let go. At the time, I would have taken a chunk of his flesh and not been sorry. Eventually, they were able to contact John—fortunately, we had a phone by this time. It took us about a year to get a phone, and it cost us about a thousand dollars.

John took me home, and I stayed in a catatonic state for a day or so, shutting the world out. I would just lie in bed, staring. I would wet the bed, and poor John had to change the sheets and me. One day a woman came to visit and said she understood my mental condition. She informed John that I was aware of everything that was going on. John was so compassionate, but he was devastated at the same time. Once, I heard him say to someone on the phone that he had to go somewhere, so when I heard the front door close, I ran to use the bathroom, so poor John wouldn't have to change the sheets again so soon. When he got back to the house, he must have thought I was dehydrated, as I hadn't had an accident for a long time. I then came to my right mind and wondered why in the world I did such crazy things.

John has seen me through five surgeries, three biopsies, and six diseases. I have had cancer, diabetes, high blood pressure, bipolar disorder, periodontal disease, and endometriosis (that cost me eight inches of my colon and my right kidney). I have no more cancer or endometriosis. My gums are now in good shape. The blood pressure, diabetes, and bipolar conditions are all controlled. I have climbed many mountains in my lifetime.

Because I tried to be the perfect wife, mother, and teacher on the mission field, I burned out after eight years of intensive work in Brazil. John and I decided it was time to return to the States, partly because of my mental exhaustion but also because we wanted our children to go to American schools. David spoke Portuguese much more than English, and so when he came back to the States at almost the age of eight, he was put in the first grade because he didn't know the English alphabet. Mary had gone to the American school in Campinas for the first one and a half years and then went to Brazilian schools. When she returned to the States, she skipped third grade because of her age. As a result of their having been in school in Brazil, they both had to have resource classes in English. This did not hurt them, as they later both graduated cum laude from the universities they attended.

It was about July 3 when I came back to my right mind after a few days being in a psychotic state. On July 5, 1980, John's brother died in a plane crash of his private plane. John had to fly back to the States for his brother's funeral. This left me alone in Brazil, trying to sell our house, furniture, and other belongings. If I thought I had stress before my breakdown, this situation was a real challenge. However, I managed to stay sane while getting ready to leave Brazil and return to the States.

John's brother had been a pilot for Braniff Airlines and also had flown B52 bombers over Vietnam. This airline gave John a free ticket to return to Brazil, but it was for standby only. John started out from Dallas, landed in Panama, and had to stay a couple of days there until he could get on another plane to continue his journey. He finally got a flight and landed in Peru. They were installing a new president in Peru, and for some reason, the officials would not allow John to leave the country. John had to stay in Lima, Peru, for four days. He had no suitcases, as they went directly on to Brazil, so he had no other clothes with him. He would call me and say he was naked because all his clothes were hanging to dry after he'd washed them. When John boarded the plane in Panama, he put his satchel, which contained five hundred dollars in cash, in the seat pocket in front of him. When he landed in Peru, he was told to get off quickly, so he forgot about that satchel. When John was walking down the street in Lima, military police followed him. At one point, John just turned around and invited them for a cup of coffee. What a confident man John was.

When John landed in Bolivia, the Bolivians were having a revolution, and people were being pulled off the plane. John went to the cockpit and told the pilot that if he got off, he wouldn't stand a chance. The pilot looked at John and said, "Sit down. We're taking off." The pilot flew out, with John sitting in the cockpit!

Then John got a flight to Paraguay, where he called me. I was thinking he would fly from Dallas to Brazil in one day, but he had spent time in Panama, Peru, Bolivia, and Paraguay! Finally, after John's odyssey throughout Central and South America, he returned to me in Campinas, Brazil. It is a wonder that I maintained my sanity during this time of extremely high stress.

We left Brazil in August 1980. Both John and I underwent hypno-analysis in November 1980. When suffering from a mental illness, one seeks various methods to heal the psyche. There are many hypnotherapists in the United States but few qualified hypno-analysts. I believe we had one of the most brilliant hypno-analysts in the country. I discovered my inscrutable subconscious mind, as the analyst and I took a journey into the recesses of my mind. Through hypnosis, he tried to take me back to the point of birth, but I did not go that far during the trance, although some people do. I was able to go into a deep sleep or hypnotic trance and wake up remembering everything. As the doctor carried me back to my childhood, I witnessed a little girl who, as he said, "did not get what she needed from her father." My father, though a good man, could not show *any* affection. I do not remember ever being hugged or held by him. This component is necessary for a child to grow and develop emotionally, but I was denied any kind of demonstrated love from my father. I don't remember my maternal grandfather ever holding or hugging me either. (My paternal grandfather died before I was born.)

What I did, then, as a result of this emotional hunger as a child, was transfer these feelings to God, my heavenly Father. That explains why, at the age of thirteen, I begged God to let me be a missionary, to serve Him in that capacity and thereby receive His affection and approval. He answered that prayer in a way that was far more than I could ask for or imagine. God gave me the most incredible mountaintop experiences one could have in life. I had the most exciting, rewarding, and fulfilling existence—it was not an easy life but a joy-filled adventure. Everything worked together for the good in my life. Even though I lacked that love from a father figure, I depended on God to love me and guide me, and so He did. This hurt and pain was all on a subconscious level. The beauty of this realization is stated in the Bible, when Jesus said, "You shall know the truth and the truth shall set you free" (John 8:32, NIV). When I found out the truth about myself, I was set free. It was like a dentist who drills through a cavity and removes all the decay from the tooth. Through hypnosis, I was able to excavate my subconscious mind, with all the hurts and pains throughout my life. We can't erase our negative experiences, but we can turn the negative events in our lives into a positive understanding and heal those core beliefs and unhealthy negative thoughts. That is how hypnosis was for me. I was hurting from a negative memory that fell into my subconscious mind and hid there until I was thirty-five, when I had my mental breakdown. Tremendous stress was the trigger for this illness. My longing for a father figure to give me the affection I needed created a drive in me so forceful that my energy was tremendous, and I sought to accomplish great things for God, my heavenly Father. When my conscious mind witnessed the subconscious, with all the hurts of an unfulfilled childhood, I then understood why I pursued certain life goals with such a strong drive. I also saw where something really bothered me but was only in my subconscious mind, and I was totally unaware of this event in my conscious mind. It was incredible!

Hypnosis is not for everybody. Many people are resistant. John was resistant, and so he was not able to go into a trance at all. I did have one painful experience with hypnosis. Sometimes when I was in a trance, the hypnotist talked to me in his deep commanding voice, and it would feel like he was taking a sharp knife and cutting every word onto the back lobe of my brain. I told him it really hurt. During hypnosis, I would wear earphones and a sleep shade like a mask over my eyes. One time I had to take the earphones off because the pain was too intense. The hypnotist said that happened sometimes. I would like to know the deeper meaning of this phenomenon. It did not happen that often.

I transferred my feelings of emotional hunger from this lack of love in my life to this analyst as a father figure; this is called transference. I "fell in love" with him after many sessions. My analyst states: "Basically, the type of relationship the psychoanalyst has with the patient is that nondescript passive relationship which permits transference to take place as a therapeutic modality." In other words, he believes transference helps the patient in therapy. John A. Scott, Sr. *Hypnoanalysis for Individual and Marital Psychotherapy,* New York, Gardner Press, Inc.,1993, page 98. I had studied a lot of psychology at the university, and I realized on an intellectual level what I was doing. Unfortunately, he suffered what is called countertransference with me, which means he "fell in love with me." For many, many years, he wanted to hear from me often. At one point, I stopped writing to him, but he wrote to me with authority and control over me, asking me to keep writing to him. I honestly believe he brainwashed me by searing his image on my brain through deep hypnosis. He gave me a cassette tape that explained all about my mental and emotional experiences from childhood, and he included on that tape that he wanted to have a relationship with me. It needs to be understood that this analyst was a leader in the church, in his fifties, with strong self-control, and had a lot of experience in dealing with emotionally needy women. As this analyst was my husband's professor at the graduate school, I remember John telling me that this professor warned the men going into this type of ministry that it was not for every man, due to the tremendous temptation to be strongly attracted to women with these type of problems and thereby succumb to sexual immorality. I spent twenty-five hours with him alone over a period of several months. During each appointment with him, I went into a deep trance. He programmed the word *sleep* on my mind, so that every time he would say, commandingly, "*Sleep*," I would go deeper and deeper into a trance, and he would penetrate my subconscious mind. At the last session, I told the doctor I wanted to wean myself from him, to forget him so I could be emotionally free and not continue to suffer this transference with him. He, as a professional, should have let me go, but instead, he insisted we keep in touch. He would send most of his letters to me where I worked, so John wasn't aware of this relationship between us.

Ms. Jan Wiener, states that "Transference is an unconscious form of projection from the patient onto the analyst and a universal phenomenon." Nonverbal and unconscious process go on continuously within the transference-counter transfer relationship. Ms. Jan Wiener, *The Therapeutic Relationship: Transference, Countertransference, and the Making of Meaning*, College Station, Texas, Texas A & M, 2009, page 12.

John was aware that I suffered transference, as he had two academic degrees in marital counseling and recognized this condition—several women had "fallen in love" with him, suffering transference through the therapy he practiced. It was really torture for me, as I believed a married Christian woman should not be thinking of another man as much as I was. I still had an emotional tie to my analyst and felt honored that he wanted to have a relationship with me. Unfortunately, he was on my mind constantly for many years. The spring of 1981 was the last time I saw this analyst. Ten years later, I called him to inform him that John had just received his doctorate degree in marriage and family counseling, as this analyst had been John's professor at the graduate school. We had been writing to each other during those ten years. He then told me on the phone, "You keep in touch, and I will keep in touch." I knew when I was in therapy with him ten years earlier that he wanted to have a relationship with me. We had developed a relationship (in mind only). This caused a lot of heartache, as I thought about him all the time, and he encouraged it. I tried to break off this relationship at different times but couldn't. This letter writing had been going on for over fifteen years. The only thing that worked was when I prayed so hard to God to release me from this man. I finally was set free, and I threw his tape and all his letters in the Dumpster. Then I wrote a stern letter to him, telling him I did not want any more correspondence with him ever again. On the day he would have received that letter, I got a phone call from a little boy, although I had no idea who he was. He didn't talk long and then hung up. I believe that was my analyst's way of saying good-bye. I never heard from him again. There are those who would say that phone call from a little boy was just a coincidence, but I believe in my heart that was his "farewell" to me.

One has to be careful in choosing a hypno-analyst or hypnotherapist. In hypnosis, there is a very strong encounter between two persons. It involves an intense emotional relationship between the hypnotist and the patient. My analyst said he penetrated me spiritually and mentally. I was so relieved when I was set free from this analyst, but I felt even more relief when I heard that he died— then I knew that he would never be able to control me or hold me in emotional bondage again. To be honest, I did all within my power to make this analyst love me, as he was my father figure. I believe I succeeded in that. I can't put the blame totally on his reaction to my attempt to attract him. He carried my burden and compassionately showed me the truth about myself with regard to my longing to be loved by my father. He literally sacrificed himself to set me free.

Love hurts. There was the pain of separation because we'd bonded together.

In May 1981, I went to see a psychiatrist. I described my symptoms and said that I had read in a magazine that a lady who had all the same symptoms as I had was given lithium, and that controlled her disorder. Lithium controls mania in bipolar disorder (formerly known as manic-depression). I took lithium for thirty years. I thank God for this cure and that God helped me to find "my marbles" once again. If I had stopped taking lithium, I would have once again experienced the ecstasy of mania and naturally would have enjoyed the highs, but I can wait until heaven to experience that ultimate joy. Dr. Fieve believes "lithium is thought to act on the cyclical aspects of mood disorders by shifting water and electrolyte (salt) levels." Dr. Ronald R. Fieve, *Moodswing,* New York, Bantam Books, Inc., 1981, page 73 In 2011, however, I had to get off lithium, as it had adversely affected my thyroid gland, and I only had one kidney. I switched to Lamictal, which has proved to control the manic highs but does not inhibit my brain, as lithium did. I could tell my creativity and inspiration were awakening. My life now is wonderful; I know I can stay within reality and still have that super-creativity and inspiration. I can stay level-headed and not have terrible mood swings.

Dr. Fieve also believes that "Compulsive gambling seems to be more frequent among the relatives of manic-depressive (bipolar) than in the general population. Manics love to gamble. They love the excitement of it. George Winokur, professor of psychology at the University of Iowa, feels that this suggest a genetic link between manic-depression and gambling. It may be similar to the link between manic-depression and alcoholism." Dr. Ronald R. Fieve, *Moodswing,* New York, Bantam Books, Inc., 1981, page 55. My younger brother is a compulsive gambler. His brain gets a high on the thrill of the challenge of gambling. Doctors now have medicine that can control this behavior so he could overcome this monster that has adversely affected much of his life, but he refuses to take anything. I admonish anyone who is diagnosed with bipolar disorder to take the medicine to be able to stay normal and reliable.

Remember that you have different options to understanding yourself. Hypnosis has the power to rewire the human mind and change people's lives for the good by focusing on living the most authentic version of you. When you fully embrace who you are, share it with others, and people will appreciate you and will flock to you effortlessly. Hypnosis gave me a deeper insight into why I did what I did and why I thought the way I thought. My subconscious mind released hidden hurts in my life to my conscious thinking. This realization enabled me to heal emotionally. I was unable to remove those memories, but I was able to understand the source of this drive that I'd had throughout most of my life.

Over the months of using hypnosis, it was like pieces of a puzzle coming together. There is a great sense of well-being in understanding oneself. Every human being grows up imperfect and thereby suffers in some way emotionally. We all have obstacles to overcome from our negative childhood events. In the back of your mind, sometimes you may wonder why you did what you did, or why you reacted or over-reacted to certain situations. Hypnosis is a wonderful tool to clear up one's past. We develop core beliefs and unhealthy memories that often settle into our subconscious mind, and this can alter the rest of our lives—unless we uncover the negativity and hurt. I believe this is what happened to both John and me in our lives. I hurt so from the lack of affection from my father that I had an intense drive to be shown love by God, and so I strove with great energy to fulfill my dream of doing mission work, to give and receive this needed element of affection and approval from God (a father figure) that was missing in my childhood. If I hadn't been hurting deeply from this lack of affection, I never would have aspired to accomplish this noble goal of mission work. Because of this drive, I was blessed by God and was able to have the most wonderful and rewarding life possible.

John, on the other hand, at the tender age of ten, was told by a very prominent preacher that he was going to hell—or at least that is how his young mind interpreted this incident. His sister still remembers the preacher's name and hearing him say those words to John. When John was a child, there were always "tent" church revivals, where those ardent preachers fiercely ranted and raved their "hell and damnation" fiery sermons that scared everyone, especially children. In John's childlike mind, he interpreted this to mean that he was doomed to hellfire forever. His subconscious mind believed this lie and influenced John's conscious mind to think that he had to do all he possibly could to please the vengeful Almighty God. John felt he had to work his way to heaven. He didn't know the loving, compassionate, and merciful Almighty God.

This powerful negative memory then settled at the bottom of John's subconscious mind, only to torment him and influence him for the following fifty-plus years. He didn't understand, consciously, why he had this enormous drive to show God he should not go to hell. We cannot remove the negative memories from our childhood, but we can learn how to understand why we interpret different experiences with a warped mind-set. If John could have seen into his subconscious mind, he would have understood why he overcompensated throughout his life and could have prevented his agony and torment.

During my illness, I had a striking experience of extreme sensitivity of all five senses, as well as with my sixth sense (intuition) and inspiration and creativity; I experienced ecstasy. I later learned that there is a part of the brain that most people never tap into. My analyst stated that I lived "on a different level than most people."

Many people take mind–altering drugs to get the effect that I got naturally. In fact, I took lithium for thirty years so that I would *not* get those highs. I also experienced the ultimate in sexual pleasure. There is a lot of misinformation and ignorance in this area with regard to the manic phase of bipolar disorder. I was faithful to my husband, but many people with bipolar disorder get very promiscuous at this stage. Instead of succumbing to every sexual urge, however, we can make the decision to follow God's laws of not committing sexual immorality. If we can control sexual urges, we can then redirect that energy to creativity and enter into a spiritual dimension. This, I believe, is what happened to me. I had many opportunities to sin against God sexually, but I did not want to sin against Him, first out of fear and then out of love for Him. My thoughts, however, were not pure many times when I was tempted. I was extremely sensitive— physically, mentally, and spiritually. I know that our minds have such potential, but few people realize or imagine this potential in all areas of their lives. This is the reason that some people experiment with drugs—they want to experience the intensity of the mind, even though that is a very dangerous road to take.

In Napoleon Hill's book, *Think and Grow Rich,* he expresses immense wisdom and knowledge about the brain, subconscious mind, faith, and higher attributes we can achieve in life. Even though this book was originally written in the 1930s, he shares some incredible ideas of developing strong character. He explains the mystery of sex in the form of transmutation. Mr. Hill defines the meaning of the word transmute. "It is, in simple language, the changing, or transferring of one element or form of energy into another. When redirected this motivating force may be used as powerful creative forces in literature, art, or in any other profession. The transmutation of sex energy calls for the exercise of willpower. But it should be given an outlet through forms of expression which enrich the body, mind, and spirit of man." *Napoleon Hill, Think and Grow Rich,* Melrose, Florida, The Ralston Society, 1937, page 185. It is switching the mind from thoughts of physical expression to thoughts of some other nature.

I believe when God created man and woman, he said it was good. My belief is that sex should be a spiritual, mental, and physical oneness between a husband and wife. Mr. Hill believes that this energy can be directed into creative and imaginative manifestations, as well as reaching the heights of spirituality.

Chapter 5
Children's Homes

Terrill Children's Home

*O*n August 1980 John took the job of Director of Social Services at Terrill Children's Home in Greenville, Texas. I was his secretary. We enjoyed working with the children and the staff there, and we made wonderful memories. John and I took a ten-day trip and toured Switzerland to celebrate my restored sanity. We experienced so much beauty in Germany, Italy, Switzerland, and Liechtenstein, the smallest country in Europe. We worked in Texas for about a year and a half.

Porter Christian Children's Home

In 1982, we moved to Oklahoma, where John was hired as the executive director of Porter Christian Children's Home. While there, John pursued the monumental task of working on his doctorate degree. Very few people, I'm convinced, would have had the tenacity to stick to this grueling project as John did, but he had drive and energy in him from his subconscious mind to attain this goal. In his childhood, he believed that his parents loved his older brother more than they loved him, so he wanted to prove to his parents that he was as good as or better than his big brother. Most people would have given up when the odds were against them; after all, John went to a two-room schoolhouse where he did not get the best education. There were so many obstacles in pursuing this degree. One of the challenges was becoming acquainted with the computer world. I had to learn all the intricacies of typing on this amazing machine. It was a very difficult time for our marriage, as the stress was extreme. I was working, did the shopping, washed clothes, cooked, and cleaned, and then typed his papers in the evenings. As long as I've known him, his motto has been "It shall be done." His doctoral degree in ministry was awarded to him in 1991. John did extensive research on burnout, showing how teachers, doctors, nurses, and others in the service areas of our population can burn out due to stress and other factors. John, however, not only wrote about burnout but 12 years later experienced it. John was the executive director at Porter Christian Home for thirteen years, from 1982 to 1995.

In the summer of 1994, our daughter, Mary, and two preachers went on a mission trip to Belarus (formerly part of the Soviet Union). When Mary returned from her mission trip, she told her dad that he must go over there and teach those beautiful people. They had been begging to study the Bible. John's first trip was in August 1994, and he fell in love with the people. He made another trip in December 1994.

Wilson Children's Home

In 1995, John was hired as the executive director at Wilson Children's Home in Memphis, Tennessee, which celebrated its seventy-fifth anniversary in 2001. President George W. Bush sent a warm, supportive letter, congratulating this institution. State senators and representatives visited there to offer congratulations.

John made many improvements to this children's home. He noticed that the gym was full of furniture and junk. He had that cleaned out and gave the gym back to the children for various activities. He put red metal roofs on the buildings and made several changes to beautify the campus. Wilson Children's Home has a farm with many kinds of animals for the kids to work with and show in the 4-H program, which helps them to learn responsibility. John built a big house at the farm for house parents who liked farm work. With approval from the board of directors, John gave land for the senior citizen center and allowed the high school athletic department to use the children's home property to develop a soccer and softball field.

I have traveled with John all over Arkansas, Tennessee, Missouri, Louisiana, and Texas while he preached and informed the supporting congregations of the wonderful work at Wilson Children's Home. His sermons have touched the hearts of all who have heard him speak. No matter how many times I heard the same stories, they still touched my heart. John—a humble man filled with so much profound character—was easily admired and respected in many parts of the world. John had incredible energy and drive to help his fellow man, and he worked well with his staff. One houseparent who was from India—I'll call her Angel—was an extremely compassionate woman with a genuine spirit. She asked John if she could take classes during the day at Memphis Tech to get her nursing degree. Angel would go to classes while her children from the cottage were in school. John allowed her to do that. Several years later, Angel was one of John's nurses when he was in the mental hospital.

John was involved in many other activities while director at Wilson Children's Home. He participated in the local Kiwanis Club, where he once served as president. He worked on many fund-raisers that helped young people receive scholarships. He was given the highest award by Kiwanis—a beautiful wall plaque that states the following: "Tablet of Honor, Kiwanis International Foundation, the name of John L. Paz is inscribed on the Tablet of Honor for service to children of the world and the citizens of Memphis and Shelby County, Tennessee." John was one of five citizens nominated for the Chamber of Commerce Citizen of the Year award.

John received another honor while at Wilson Children's Home, when in August 2002, the governor of Tennessee appointed him to the State Child Abuse and Neglect Prevention Board.

John was very active in foreign mission work during his time as director of Wilson Children's Home. From 1994 through 2002, John made nine humanitarian/mission trips to Borisov, Belarus. In order to enter this extremely poor country, John and the others traveling with him would take in diabetic and other medical supplies. When John presented the doctor with boxes of catheters, the doctor was very excited, as he had been using one catheter over and over again. John baptized several people there, taught classes, visited with influential doctors, and visited high schools. He touched their hearts and souls, and these Russians came to love this compassionate American Christian.

One reason I never wanted to go to Belarus with John was because of the terrible Chernobyl nuclear reactor accident on April 25, 1986. That released extensive amounts of radiation all over Europe but especially over Belarus, and 135,000 people had to be evacuated. Many cancer deaths ultimately were attributed to the disaster, and John saw many children who were dying there because of being exposed to that huge amount of radiation. Americans who went there were warned not to drink the milk, yet John ate a lot of sour cream that the women piled on his pancakes. John was so unselfish that he did not let the fear of radiation stop him from sharing the Gospel, and he didn't want to offend the ladies who made these pancakes for him. I am afraid I was weak in both faith and in courage and could not overcome this fear. God protected John yet again. I was planning to make the trip with him to Belarus for his tenth time, but John had his breakdown before we could go. I do regret that I never made at least one of those trips with him to have shared in that fulfilling experience.

The story must be told about a young lady I will call Lena. During John's second trip to Belarus, he went with Pete, a man from Ft. Smith, Arkansas. The ladies of the church gave John and Pete an encouraging note for each day, to uplift them while they were in Europe. As John dressed one morning in Borisov, he put an encouraging card in his shirt pocket for that day. The card had flowers on one side and a quote from Abraham Lincoln on the other side. That particular day, the Russians invited Pete to visit a military site, and John was invited to visit a mental hospital. When John walked in the hospital, he saw a lovely, blonde, eighteen-year-old girl crying. She never stopped crying the whole time he was there. He noticed there were no medicines in the hospital; they used only hypnosis for treatment. John was able to meet this young woman, Lena. The interpreter explained that Lena was an orphan who lived with her alcoholic grandmother. She was in the mental hospital because of her severe depression. So many of the people there had no hope, and alcoholism ran rampant. John brought hope to them in so many ways.

At this time, John could not really understand her depression, but years later, he would face firsthand that awful state of being. John was so touched by her human misery that he remembered he had an encouraging card in his pocket. He took that card and gave it to her, along with an invitation to come to the library the next day where they were having Bible studies. He never thought that she would come but to his amazement, the next day she arrived with the card in her hand. Still crying, she asked, "What does this say?" The interpreter translated it for her. Many of the interpreters were former KGB agents who had been converted to Christ. Their English was very good. John then pointed out to Lena that in Matthew 19:29, the Bible explains that even though she was an orphan, by following Christ she could have other mothers, fathers, sisters, and brothers. Lena stopped crying. John never saw her cry again. The day before John and Pete left to return to the States, they gave a banquet for those who studied with them. Lena attended the banquet with hope in her heart, mind, and soul. John said, "Either her medicine kicked in"—he was joking, as they did not have medicines for depression—"or God's Word touched her soul."

Several years later on one of John's trips to Belarus, he tried to find Lena to continue studying with her. Some of the men tried to discourage him from looking for her, and he finally found out why— she was a Jew, and they were prejudiced against Jews. John went to a well-to-do neighborhood and was able to locate her, her husband, and her four-year-old son. Through Lena's eyes, John could see her hunger for God's Word. He wanted so much to share the good news with her and her family, but her husband was trying to protect her from American religious groups that were confusing them. John could only give her little boy a children's Bible. It is our hope that Lena has read the truth over and over to her young son and thereby understands Jesus' love for her and what she must do to be saved.

A few years earlier, on a day when the library in Borisov was open, which was where John and the other missionaries held Bible studies, a middle-aged woman came to join the Bible study. She explained to John, through the interpreter, that she had seen the New Testament but had never seen the Old Testament. She was so excited when John gave some preliminary information about the Old Testament and then let her read the first three chapters of Genesis. She read on and on and did not want to stop. The next day, John gave her a spare Bible. She was so elated that her joy filled the room. Can you imagine life without knowing about the creation, the Psalms, David, Moses, or Abraham? I have given many Bibles to people in Brazil who previously had not owned one. There are few joys greater than that. Shortly after one of John's last visits, the government of Belarus forbade open Bible studies. They had a Communist president who did not permit open religious assemblies. They continued studies, however, in private homes at their own risk.

These are just a few of the many stories where the Gospel was carried across the ocean to a land that did not know God. I believe when John sees those Russian brothers and sisters in heaven, it will warm his soul for eternity. On John's last trip to Belarus in 2002, I wrote a poem about him:

> My dear John holds much love for the Belarusian people in his heart; this is why for the ninth time we must be apart. I must share him so that he can share Christ to the lost and show them the way to the cross. The days roll on and people come and go. I look forward to John returning, but time runs slow. He will come back so full of enthusiasm and content to know that God has used him to help a foreign people and what that has meant. He carried medicines to the diabetics and those in pain. He carried toys and

gifts until his suitcases were bulging on the plane. I've thought of how he has dedicated his life to helping mankind. He has on three continents diligently trod, carrying in his heart and soul the Word of God, trying to lift humanity one soul at a time, *this man of mine*!

Brazilian Children's Home

In 1997, several of us made a survey trip to Rio de Janeiro to visit the orphanage. Two of the men who went to Brazil reported to the other board members of Wilson Children's Home, regarding the possibility of sponsoring and partially supporting the Brazilian home. On June 1, 1998, Wilson Children's Home assumed the sponsorship of the LAR Cristao (the Christian children's home in Brazil). The owners of the hacienda in the state of Sao Paulo came to the United States and met with the board of directors of Wilson Children's Home. In 1999, they sold their seven-bedroom, seven-bathroom house, along with another six acres, to be turned into the children's home. The house also included a swimming pool and tennis courts and was sold for about one-fourth of the value. Funds were secured both in Brazil and the States and from a foundation to buy their farm. This was in the city of Cabreuva, Sao Paulo. The children loved their new surroundings. One day a little boy was lying on the ground, looking up at the sky. When John asked what he was doing, the little boy said he was watching the clouds. In Rio, the smog was so bad that the children hardly ever saw a clear sky. It was a joy for him to watch the fluffy white clouds drifting by.

As was mentioned, John worked with the president of the board back in 1972 when this young man was an adolescent at the Christian camp. Thirty years later, this man became president of the board of directors. This is a very noble and needed mission work. Many churches and individuals in the States are supporting the LAR. I have visited the Lar in Cabreuva, Brazil, several times. John had been so instrumental in developing this whole project. Many would say it's impossible to take on the sponsorship of a children's home on another continent. John knows that nothing is impossible for God, because "it is no secret what God can do."

Chapter 6
The Albanian Connection

*I*n 1998, there was a lot of unrest and political upheaval in the country of Albania. Parents were feverishly trying to get their senior high school children out of the country. Wilson Children's Home was approached by an organization in California that worked with a foreign exchange program and asked if we would take some of these students. We were led to believe that all these students were seniors in high school, but five of them already had graduated. Parents wanted to get them out of the country. Seven young people came to our campus. Five of them claimed to be Muslim. Two were Christian (although some students indicated they were Muslim because they feared persecution if they indicated they were Christian). They were to start school at the Manzano Senior High School in Memphis. Mimi, one of the Albanian girls, arrived in the States two days after her father was shot and killed. For six weeks, they really enjoyed school, and the teachers loved them. We also took two Chinese boys on an emergency basis, but they could barely speak English, and they soon moved to Texas. The school had a lot of problems with these two Chinese boys while they were there, so after six weeks, the school announced that the Albanian students had to be expelled, citing their policy of only accepting six foreign students a year—they said they were past their quota. This problem stirred up a hornet's nest, first in Memphis and then in the entire United States. The Associated Press took the story all over the country, and soon lawyers from New York, Texas, and even California started calling us. A lawyer in New York, offered to donate his time to helping these students and gave me many suggestions for resolving this situation. The story also appeared in the prestigious national magazine *Education Week.*

A lawyer from Memphis came to our rescue. John often worked day and night to obtain documentation that would allow the students to remain in the United States and to get them enrolled in Southeast Christian College in Memphis, a two-year college at the time. He helped two of the students get their GEDs (the equivalent of a high school diploma), went through all kinds of red tape to get their proper documentation, and did all the paperwork so they might go to a Christian college and not be deported. By the grace of God, all seven were enrolled in Southeast Christian College by January 1999.

Anton, who was the oldest Albanian student, told me that in 1995, Osama Bin Laden came to Albania to recruit followers. I had a feeling that Anton was one of the followers who went to hear Osama speak, because when 9/11 happened, Anton showed no remorse and actually acted like the United States got what it deserved.

Anton had stolen money from the children's home and had been defiant and rebelled against our authority. He really scared me. After the spring semester in 2002, Anton went back to Albania for a visit. When he tried to return to the United States, he was unable to get a visa to enter the country to continue college. He tried to re-enter for about eighteen months but was denied, as he was from a country that was sympathetic to Bin Laden. One Sunday morning in the fall of 2003, Anton showed up in our backyard. I was alone in the house, as John had gone to preach out of town. I was afraid of Anton and did not want to answer the door, but I was on my way to church. When I asked him how he got back into the United States, he said he sneaked back in with a group of professionals who were flying to Miami for just a stopover. I asked him if he'd seen Bin Laden again, and he wouldn't answer me. I had a strong feeling that Anton was possibly a terrorist.

He told me he was going to go visit his "cousin" in Naples, Florida, instead of going back to college. He left her address with me in case he received any mail at our house, so I then could forward it to him in Florida. It didn't make sense to me that he arrived in Miami and then came all the way to my house in Memphis, just to give me his forwarding address and then go to Naples, Florida. Several people were concerned that he was dangerous.

Even before Anton left to go back to Albania for a visit, many of us became suspicious that he could be a terrorist. I wrote to the FBI to have them check on him, as he was a true Muslim and had said and done some things that would indicate he might be a threat. My co-worker said if I didn't contact the FBI, he would. Before I contacted the FBI, I found his cousin's name and address in Florida on the Internet, but a few weeks after I notified the FBI, that cousin's name and address had disappeared from the Internet. Something happened.

We never heard what happened to Anton—whether he was jailed, deported, or what. One of the other Albanian boys said he knew where Anton was, but he wouldn't tell anybody.

After the students attended Southeast Christian College, four of them transferred to Barker Christian University in Memphis, and one transferred to Smith Christian University in Little Rock,

Arkansas. One of the girls, Mimi, only attended college for about a year and then she moved to England to go to art school.

Eventually, two Muslim girls were baptized into Christ. Their statements are noteworthy. Leona stated, "I am very thankful to all of you and to Wilson Children's Home for giving me the opportunity to get to know God and our Savior, Jesus. Being at Barker Christian University is a blessing for me, because I'm together with brothers and sisters in Christ who are great examples for me."

Ester typed an entire page; here is just part of what she said: "I am reading twenty chapters of the New Testament every night. I feel so wonderful and calm because I feel God so near to me. ... I was wondering if Dr. Paz can baptize me. ... You and Dr. Paz changed my life ... brought me in the right way to know God so that He could touch my heart in the most perfect way. I feel so blessed by God. ... I think it is coming the time for me to be His child. I thank Him every single night that I am here and that I have the opportunity to be with Christians. I thank Him for bringing me to Memphis so that He could show me His way. I thank Him for Dr. Paz and Joy that helped me to go through the most difficult year of my life, for being there, crying with me when my daddy died." Ester is a former Muslim who really knew nothing about God in her country.

Ester graduated cum laude from Barker Christian University in May 2002, earning a degree in international business. John performed her wedding ceremony the week after her graduation. She and her husband, Pete, and twin daughters now live in San Diego, California. This couple bought their own home, and Pete works for the government. Ester's brother and mother have both come over to the States from Albania and were taught the Gospel. John baptized them too. Her brother, Artur, is a doctor and lived in New York City during his residency in anesthesiology. He now practices in Palm Springs, California.

Leona returned to her home in Albania, where she works for the American embassy. Leona's mother was converted to Christ in Albania. These people can influence and teach their relatives and friends. The ripple effect goes on throughout time.

Ariel graduated from Barker Christian University in May 2002. She lives in Austin, Texas, where she teaches art. She married an American.

Arturo also graduated from Barker Christian University and lives in Amarillo, Texas. The last Albanian student, Nathan, graduated from Smith Christian University. Nathan planned on going back to his country as a missionary. He was a Bible and psychology major. These new Christians can spread the Gospel to their Muslim friends and relatives in Albania. Here again I say, "It is no secret what God can do." I believe many people will be converted to Christ throughout the world because John thought it worthwhile to expend so much time, money, and energy on these Albanian students. The more Muslims we can convert to Christianity, the better off the whole world will be. I believe that John had the positive aspect of bipolar disorder for many years, which was that drive and energy that he used to help so many people around the world. He actually convinced the board of directors to fund the project of sending the Albanian young people to three different private universities for four years. That cost a lot of money. Very few people would have gone to the lengths that John did to help so many people.

Chapter 7
The Agony

*O*n May 2002, John made his ninth humanitarian/mission trip to Belarus, which involved a lot of stress. It was extremely challenging to get the invitation to Belarus, because the Communist government made it more difficult to get a visa. John had to get all the medical supplies, such as diabetic supplies for children, and other hospital supplies to take to the Russians. He had to raise more funds from the different churches to finance the trip. This trip to Belarus was stressful alone, but then the very next month, in June, we took a vacation and went on a cruise to Alaska. In July 2002, John and I made a trip to Brazil with a team of several teachers to put on a vacation Bible school. This also was very stressful for John, because he felt responsible for this team of fifteen people. John and I were the only ones who spoke Portuguese, so we had to do a lot of translating. In August 2002, John was alone for ten days while I spent that time in Oklahoma visiting our daughter. For the entire year of 2002, John had trouble with insomnia, which gave him only a few hours of sleep a night.

When I returned from Oklahoma, John had developed a terrible problem—obsessive/compulsive behavior. He cleaned out drawers and vacuumed the entire house. He would go to bed at 8:30 at night but get up at 11:30 and work the rest of the night—and then work all day. He was on an agitated, manic high, and I recognized the signs of the manic phase of bipolar disorder, as I had suffered from the same mania with this illness.

John was completely stressed out before his illness. He had put every ounce of effort into taking care of Wilson Children's Home, the Brazilian home, the Albanian students, the Belarusian people, and board members of two organizations. He was on the Governor's Council against child abuse, a leader of the church, and on and on. When the economy and the stock markets suffered in 2008, that affected the children's home in a big way, as some churches and individuals had to cut their support, which made it a constant financial struggle to make ends meet. All that stress took its toll. I tried to point out to John that he was doing too much. The more I told him that, the more he took on other projects. He was like a runaway train.

I went to his family doctor and pleaded with him to give John lithium, which he did. Within two weeks of taking the medication, John started sleeping all night again. He completely stopped the obsessive/compulsive behavior and came down from his high. He was cured of all three of these symptoms after two weeks on lithium. The doctor told me emphatically to make sure that John took his antidepressant medication, as he knew that John could go from the manic to the depressive cycle of this disorder. That first antidepressant, trazodone, made him groggy, so he stopped taking it.

In January 2003, John started seeing a psychiatrist. He put John on a different antidepressant, Lexapro. Without my knowledge, John stopped taking it. The warning label on the medication reads: "Do not stop taking this, as you could go into a deep depression." That is exactly what happened. John fell into the deepest, blackest depression; he could not even talk, just like I could not talk when I was suffering with this illness.

In February 2003, I checked John into the hospital in Memphis, where he stayed for sixteen days. By coincidence or divine intervention, the very compassionate Angel, who had worked for John at Wilson Children's Home and studied nursing while there, was one of John's nurses. She looked right at John and said in her cute accent, "Dr. Paz, it is because of you that I am here today!" She took special care of him. With her kindness, she was able to get John to eat, take medicine, and sleep. John was so paranoid that he refused to eat, because he thought somebody was poisoning the food. For about two weeks, the psychiatrist tried several types of medication to no avail. When he then tried Risperdal, John finally responded to and was allowed to return home. He was cured of hearing voices and his paranoia.

Words cannot describe the incredible pain, torment, and agony that we both went through during his illness. He lost fifty pounds in the first six months. For the next few years, he had his good days and bad days. I kept telling him that someday he would be able to help others who also struggled with this disorder—and that is one of the goals of this writing, to help others who do not understand what is happening to them or their loved ones and to give them hope.

We will always be thankful to the board of directors for standing by John and putting him on administrative leave with pay. I believe in the last year before his illness, he worked night and day and just burned out. As I mentioned, John's doctoral thesis was on burnout. As John stated: "Burnout is a syndrome of emotional exhaustion and cynicism that occurs frequently among those who work with people problems; the condition is characterized by a sense of emotional depletion, resulting in feeling one cannot give any longer at a psychological level."

The list of symptoms for such people as childcare workers, doctors, and nurses who are approaching burnout include exhaustion, fatigue, headaches or somatic complaints, increased drug or alcohol use, sleep disturbances, and lethargic feelings. Emotional symptoms could include loss of enthusiasm and crying, feelings of helplessness and depression, or a quickness to become angry. Burnout is also described as a feeling that one has failed or is exhausted because of the constant contact with people who are making demands on one's strength and emotional resources. So many demands were made on John for so many years that he eventually succumbed to burnout.

As I've mentioned, when I was living in Brazil, I felt that it was a sin for a Christian to be depressed. When I was thirty-four years old, however, I went through three months of deep depression. I learned there was such a thing as a chemical imbalance. John went through fifty-seven years of his life without knowing what depression was, and then he struggled with depression himself. One therapist said that John actually burned out the neurotransmitters in his brain, and that would take time to heal.

I believe things happen for a reason. I also believe that the Lord can use us to help other people with bipolar disorder. There is still much ignorance in this country regarding this condition. Many times, people are misdiagnosed with bipolar disorder when it is some other mental illness, such as schizophrenia. Other times, people with bipolar disorder are misdiagnosed with such things as fibromyalgia or other illnesses. The great actress, Patty Duke, suffered for a period of time with this disorder. Her doctor did not know what was wrong at first, but then he finally diagnosed her with bipolar disorder. She took lithium. She has gone on talk shows and written articles for magazines to get the word out about this illness. I have read two of her books. People with bipolar disorder often go into show business, as when they are in the manic phase, they are very witty and creative.

My story is a success story, because even though I suffered with bipolar disorder, I took the necessary medication that allowed me to live a normal life. Lithium served me well, but I realize lithium is not for everybody. Still, a lot of medicines on the market can control this disorder—Tegretol, Depakote, and Lamictal, for example. Life can truly be beautiful with the help of the right drugs. Doctors sometimes need to try several before they find the right one. Every person is different, so be patient and work with the doctor. John's psychotherapist and his psychiatrist in Memphis both were appalled that John had taken so many medications. He took one strong antipsychotic, risperidone, for seven years, but his therapist said he should only have taken it for a couple of months and said that John might have permanent damage because of the medicines he'd taken.

As the therapist explained to us, be aware that each state has its own set of regulations with regard to the drugs prescribed to a patient, but it's not necessarily what is best for the patient. In Tennessee, the doctors gave John a type of antidepressant that psychiatrists in other states did not use.

I write this to show all that God did through us, even though we were bipolar. I write this to give hope to those who are in despair over their particular situation. Many people have helped me through their books or seminars. Always remember, "It is no secret what God can do. What He has done for others, He will do for you!"

John suffered his mental breakdown in February 2003. He has taken at least twenty-four different psychotropic medications over ten years. In the fall of 2003, John's psychiatrist encouraged him to try the electroconvulsive treatments (ECT), formerly known as electric shock treatments. With ECT, the doctor puts the patient to sleep and causes a seizure in the brain. These treatments are effective most of the time. The doctor informed us that ECT does help a lot of people with depression. After John took six of the treatments and wasn't responding to them, however, the doctor informed me that he would shock John's entire brain bilaterally, instead of just one-half of the brain. The seventh treatment was done bilaterally, but John still didn't respond. Then, after the eighth ECT, John was depression-free for one whole day. After the ninth treatment, John had a tremendous loss of memory, but was depression-free for twelve days. The doctor assured me that in about six weeks, John would regain his memory. John then started taking a new medication, Lamictal, which is supposed to keep the depression from coming back. I talked with several patients who were having ECT treatments, and they all told me how much good the treatments were doing for their depression, but it did not work for John.

John's father died in March 2004, and John slipped into a depression that he couldn't seem to shake. I then learned of a new procedure that the FDA approved in 2005—a device called vagus nerve implant therapy. A vagus nerve stimulator has been used for years to treat epilepsy, but it also is used to fight depression for those people who are resistant to all other forms of treatment. John was definitely in this category. The device is a pacemaker-like implant. Wires snake up the neck to the vagus nerve, delivering tiny electric shocks through that nerve and into the brain. Depression often accompanies epilepsy, and some doctors have reported that epileptic patients who used this vagus nerve device felt happier, even if the implant failed to reduce their seizures. The vagus nerve leads to a region of the brain that's thought to play a role in mood. John's doctor strongly encouraged him to try this device. Although this has helped many depressed people, unfortunately, John didn't respond to it—the thirty-thousand-dollar implant did not help at all.

In our pursuit of healing, John and I tried many things. I was always looking for information that might help. Bipolar disorder is a hot topic in the country today. Researchers are finding out that many children diagnosed as having ADHD may really be bipolar. Seminars on bipolar disorder take place across the country. One such seminar I attended in Little Rock, given by a doctor whose mother was bipolar. He was a diplomat candidate in psychopharmacology. He offered so much knowledge on bipolar disorder. I have read many enlightening books on this topic, as I've tried to understand all I could about how John's and my brains were wired.

Chapter 8
Suicide Attempt

On September 13, 2010, Dr. Mendoza changed John's medication, taking him off Klonopin, an addictive drug, and Tegretol and putting him on Buspar. However, John had withdrawal symptoms so bad that I took him to the hospital on September 19. He was treated for five hours with blood tests, urine tests, and an electrocardiogram. For the longest time, they couldn't lower his anxiety. The doctors kept increasing the dosage of the anti-anxiety medicine Ativan and then added Valium. He was then sent home. He had been staying in bed about twenty hours a day—he simply could not face life.

On September 23, 2010, John became suicidal when the doctor took him off the addictive drug too fast. I had to call 911. I had to take a knife out of his hand. He went down to the basement, looking for the guns, but I'd hidden them earlier so he didn't know where they were. He got a couple of plastic bags and put a string around his throat—he tried any way he could to end this hell on earth. After this episode, I sold his guns and bought him a recliner. He was in a catatonic state. I could see such torment and agony in his eyes—his anxiety was extreme.

The first police officer to respond to my 911 call told John to turn over on his stomach, as he was just staring into space. John didn't obey the officer, so the officer used a taser on him twice at close range. This officer clearly did not know anything about mental illness. There was a small puddle of blood on the carpet from this action. I was told that the blood tests the next day showed John's liver enzymes were affected by being hit with a taser. Firemen, ambulances, and police all responded to the 911 call. After about a half hour, John was taken by ambulance to St. Mary's Hospital in Memphis. He never said a word during this whole ordeal. When I went to see John at the hospital, a guard stood outside his door, and he was strapped down on the bed. I tried to comfort him, but he didn't talk to me either. I visited for some time with the social worker and gave her a lot of information. The next day John was transported by ambulance to Cedar Adventist Hospital in Nashville. All the staff in the geriatric psychiatric unit ward were so helpful and patient.

When John entered the hospital, he was about as low as a human can get; he was delirious. Dr. Angelo D. Christian, the geriatric psychiatrist, started John on the necessary medications—Geodon, Ativan, and Zyprexa—and after a few days, he was much better. The doctor encouraged John to start ECT treatments and after just a couple of weeks, John was completely free of depression and anxiety and was in his right mind. He was, in many ways, like he was years before his depression.

I want to encourage anyone who is resistant to all treatments that there is hope for even the worst cases. Dr. Christian was my hero. His expertise and knowledge so impressed me, along with his kind and compassionate heart. John has had at least five other psychiatrists in three states. After eight years of turmoil, agony, hopelessness, and much prayer, God performed a miracle through this brilliant doctor. People kept telling me that John would be depressed until he died. I was about to give up hope when this angel of a doctor touched John's life with healing and brought him up from the abyss of darkness to the light of mental health.

John stayed six weeks in the hospital. He was released on November 4, 2010. He continued taking ECT treatments on an outpatient basis for a few weeks. These last treatments did not help. John was cured of his terrible anxiety and was in his right mind, but his depression returned. The doctor tried Ritalin, but that caused John to be so nervous that he had to discontinue it after ten days.

In May 2011, the doctor started John on gabapentin. For the first two weeks, it seemed to help, but on the third week, as the dosage was increased, John had terrible, invasive thoughts. He heard voices cursing God day and night, so this was extreme torment for John, as he loved God and his whole life was about serving the Lord. The doctor took John off gabapentin and put him back on Ativan. John still remained in agony from extreme depression, and he felt so guilty from hearing those invasive thoughts, but these thoughts ceased.

On July 29, at my request, the doctor started slowly taking John off Zyprexa and replaced it with risperidone, as I thought the Zyprexa was causing some of his depression. During the entire month of August 2011, John's mind deteriorated so fast that he became debilitated. He started getting rebellious, sneaky, and at times had a sinister look on his face that scared me. I had to shave, bathe, and help him dress. He lost some of his memory and was like a zombie many times. He was completely mentally ill, so I had to put him into an assisted living home, which broke my heart, but I was completely exhausted from caring for him. If I ruined my health, our daughter would have had to take care of both of us. Before placing him in assisted living, I was homebound, because I could not leave him for a minute. If I would be gone from the bedroom for ten minutes to fix his breakfast, he would have all his clothes off by the time I returned and be getting ready to take another shower—he was out of his mind. In September 2011, I placed him in the Presbyterian Assisted Home, where he stayed for four months, and it cost me over twelve thousand dollars.

Presbyterian Assisted Home was really very nice, and the workers were very compassionate. John found his mission there, as he studied the Bible with the workers and the residents. There were only seven residents in a regular house in a nice neighborhood close to the mountains. He seemed to enjoy being with other people. He was improving.

Changing John to the drug risperidone was what caused him to be completely irrational. This medicine made him extremely mentally ill. He stopped taking risperidone as soon as he arrived at the assisted home, and when Dr. Christian put John back on Zyprexa, he returned to his right mind and was not a problem. He continued to be nervous and depressed, but his mind was rational. Even though Dr. Christian was the best psychiatrist John had, John absolutely refused to go see him in Nashville. Since 2003, John had been filled with negativity and severe depression. He was obsessed with worry about the least little things; he had dread, agony, fear, and so many other negative thoughts. His mental health was a disaster. On November 7, 2011, John started seeing a new psychiatrist, Dr. McDaniel, in Memphis.

I brought John back home from the assisted living home on January 7, 2012, as he was in his right mind, but he still had anxiety and depression. In February 2012, Dr. McDaniel prescribed a new drug recently approved by the FDA called Viibryd. John had such bad side effects from this medicine, however, that he had to stop taking it within a few days. In May 2012, Dr. McDaniel said he would take John off Zyprexa gradually, but he prescribed too low of a dose too soon, and John started having hallucinations at night. I realized then that he needed this antipsychotic drug to maintain sanity—he was in a serious mental meltdown. I increased his dosage, and he showed some improvement. The doctor had made a big mistake—we all make mistakes, but this could have been disastrous for John.

Before the age of fifty-seven, John was a compassionate, kind, loving, sensitive, caring, focused, ambitious, positive person, with a drive to excel. He had no destructive emotions prior to succumbing to this illness. He was driven by extraordinary energy to accomplish so many amazing achievements. After age fifty-seven, John experienced hell on earth, as he would describe his life. John's whole attitude and view on life was so negative and full of emotions such as deep depression, anxiety, nervousness, being lost, despair, worry, sorrow, discouragement, guilt, dread, fear, humiliation, feeling overwhelmed, insecurity, helplessness, hopelessness, low self-esteem, confusion, defensiveness, grief, frustration, panic, conflict, terror, feeling wishy-washy, shame, loneliness, and worthlessness. John had none of these destructive emotions prior to succumbing to this illness. Lurking in his subconscious, however, was a whole scary new world. At times, he would say that the devil was after him. I believe John really was in a spiritual war. There was a battle between good and evil. Every day he would keep the "spiritual sword"—the Bible, God's Word—close to him. He knew he needed strength that could only come from his Creator.

John overcompensated all his life with tremendous amounts of energy to fulfill an incredible number of accomplishments. John's drive continued year after year because in his subconscious mind was that dreadful, negative emotion that literally scared the hell out of him, and it was calling the shots on his conscious mind. He believed a lie at the age of ten and thought he was going to hell, so he did everything humanly possible to avoid this terrible fate. He thought he could work his way into heaven—another false belief, because no one can work his or her way to heaven. It's by God's grace, mercy, and love, along with obedience to Christ, that we are promised an eternal home.

John's sickness began in the fall of 2002, and as of this writing in 2013, it's been ten years of the most intense despair, agony, and torment. John started to withdraw more and more into a mental illness retreat, into deeply hurting depression. He would say his heart hurt. He struggled to live, and he feared to die. What a state of pure torment.

For my part, having to live day by day with someone I have loved and with whom I have shared a glorious and rewarding life for thirty-six years and then having to suffer for many years also was so torturous. I, as his wife and caregiver, have had to build a wall around my heart, soul, and mind to protect myself from all the pain I had to endure while watching helplessly as my loved one traveled this road of heartbreaking torment. I knew, however, that this would end someday, if not here on earth then when at death he would be set free. John could not face what drove him to his despair and torment. He realized intellectually that he was running from the truth and that his subconscious was controlling his conscious mind. Yet he did not know how to unlock the truth that he was so hurt emotionally and spiritually as a child. He had self-sabotaging emotional barriers. At times, he said he was tired and could not take it anymore. The fact that his physical health and immune system were so strong was amazing, as many doctors and therapists see the results of such debilitating depression on the immune system, which can weaken and cause all kinds of physical stress and diseases. This was not true with John. He rarely got sick physically; he had a strong constitution.

I now realize there are some things worse than death. I hate to admit it, but I was hoping that if John could not get well that he would go on to his heavenly reward. I believed that in his physical death that he would find that peace, joy, contentment, love, and complete awareness of the insane struggles that had tormented him in this life and thus be set free. I also realized that it was not up to me to heal John. There was tremendous pain in watching John writhing in mental, emotional, and spiritual despair. I tried everything I knew to awaken his conscious mind to the lies and despair that his subconscious mind was putting him through but for some reason, he could not face the truth about himself.

I want to encourage everyone to never give up hope. Be realistic and realize that in this life, there will be suffering as well as joy and peace. The only thing that has given me joy in the midst of all this pain is my faith in God. I lived on a daily diet of the Psalms, and the entire Bible sustained me as God gave me strength, comfort, peace, endurance, and a joy that rose above the madness in our world. I experienced the peace that passes all understanding. Life really is short, but there is the belief that if we walk with God and obey Jesus, we have the hope of an indescribable eternal life, with all-encompassing, unconditional love, joy, and peace. This knowledge, wisdom, and understanding has inspired me all my life, and I want to help others who are going through this agony with a loved one to know there is hope, if not in this life then in the next—life eternal.

I found many helpful avenues to encourage, strengthen, and guide me as a caregiver. One example is that I ordered several healing CDs that helped my mind meditate on a deeper level of consciousness. I ordered these CDs from the Jim Oliver Music website, www.jimolivermusic.

com. The soothing sounds of the harp and other instruments give me an indescribable peace. I constantly pray to my heavenly Father and to Jesus for strength and fortitude, and these prayers have been granted. There is a big picture here that I cannot see, but I know who can see it, and He directs me through this maze of mental illness that I am experiencing with John. Some may say that they are amazed that I could "put up" with this for so long. However, when I remember the profound gentleness and love John had for me when I suffered my breakdown, it gives me fortitude to carry on. I dealt with a great man who lost his mind, hope, and drive. We "danced" on three continents of this world. We laughed a lot and loved a lot. All in all, life has been an incredible journey in this marriage.

As of this writing, John is still in the pits of depression. I don't believe that any more medicines would help. Now he is on anti-depressant, anti-anxiety and antipsychotic medicine, but John has what is called TRD—treatment-resistant depression. We've tried everything we know for him to conquer his depression—medications, ECT, vagus nerve implant, and many therapists—but so far he hasn't been able to overcome. It has been an awful burden for him to carry the weight of this depression for ten years. I am reminded of the dream I had in which I had to see myself as I really was. I had to recognize my weaknesses and face my demons. I was able to look into my subconscious mind and be set free. I told John that he too had to face who he is to be set free.

I also believe that what all we experienced with bipolar disorder can help other struggling people to see themselves as they really are and to rise above all the self-limiting, self-sabotaging, negative, false core beliefs that they have suffered. In doing this, we can have a joy-filled life without limits, and with God's help, we can climb that mountain.

Chapter 9
Genealogy

I did a study of our family tree and found many relatives who suffered depression and several who were suicidal; one cousin did commit suicide. Those who succumb to bipolar disorder can see from their family tree that many of their relatives suffered depression or manic behavior. John's family also shows many relatives who suffered depression and manic behavior—his father, brother, three sisters, and an uncle. In October 2012, his nephew who suffered from bipolar disorder committed suicide because he wouldn't take his medicine as he should have done. I believe that psychiatric tools, including medication, healing methods, and diet, can help maintain sanity in most people.

Some people may wonder if our children have bipolar disorder, as it is hereditary. They have a 40 percent chance of getting this condition, as both John and I have it. Our children have been very stable and successful so far. This can skip several generations.

Our daughter, Mary, started doing mission work in Brazil when she was ten. When we had a campaign, she would translate and hand out brochures with the campaigners—students from US Christian universities. These students would depend on Mary and other missionary children to interpret for them and help them to find the right bus in the city to get to their destination. When Mary grew up, she graduated cum laude from Barker Christian University, majoring in English. Mary took advantage of studying for one semester in Florence, Italy, where the university has a villa. There was a lot of stress in that situation. She traveled all over Europe to ten countries. Later, Mary taught two years on an Indian reservation. As was mentioned, she went on a two-week mission trip to Belarus and taught the children and a ladies class. After teaching the Navajo Indian children for two years, Mary joined an Italian mission group called Avanti Italia that is sponsored by a church in Memphis. She moved to Florence, Italy, learned the Italian language, and did mission work there for about a year and a half. She taught English using the Bible. She has done mission work on three continents.

After about a year and a half in Italy, Mary was running out of money, as she was paying back student loans, so she returned to the States to teach English as a second language in Oklahoma City. She teaches students from Korea, Japan, Germany, and other countries from all over the world. Mary has studied five foreign languages and is tri-lingual. She also put in many hours, working with her congregation in the World Bible School mission work. Mary has encountered a lot of stress but so far shows no signs of bipolar disorder.

Our son, David, was born in Sao Paulo, Brazil, in 1972. When he was three months old, he nearly died of dehydration. I stayed up with him for twenty-two hours, giving him lifesaving liquid every ten minutes around the clock, as the doctor instructed, so he would not dehydrate. He would just cry and cry. I felt so helpless, and my dear mother was a continent away, so I couldn't ask her for help. I realized that it was humanly impossible to keep David alive, so I prayed to God, trying to bargain with Him that if He would let David live, then I would never let him forget that he belonged to God. The doctor told me if I could get David to the States, he might live, because the climate in Brazil kills babies there in the hot summer. The next day, plans were made for me to take David and Mary to the States. It was a real hassle to take a Brazilian boy out of the country. I had to have John's written permission, and the authorities interrogated us thoroughly. The military police weren't about to give up a Brazilian male child easily. Finally, they let us go.

When we arrived in Dallas on the other side of the equator, it was winter and very cold. David looked like a wrinkled-up little old man because he was so dehydrated. The doctor in Dallas said they never give babies penicillin that young. Now he is deathly allergic to penicillin. Within a few days, David started thriving, and he has been in good health ever since. I reminded David throughout the years that God let him live, so he belonged to God. As a result, he has lived in a way that his life reflects this realization. David was diagnosed with dyslexia in third grade, and so he had to overcome many obstacles. (I was shocked when he quoted a lengthy passage of Shakespeare when he was a junior in high school. His teacher told me that David compensated for his reading disability.) Despite these obstacles, David graduated cum laude from a Christian university, majoring in math. During his years at the university, on spring breaks he would fly up to Minnesota with a team and do mission work. He also spent one whole summer in Minnesota, working with the preacher and sharing the Gospel. David has spent several summers as a Christian camp counselor also. David taught math for thirteen years at a Christian high school and was head coach for a girl's volleyball team. This was not just a sport to David; he treated it as teaching his girls how to develop a relationship with God and develop character, as well as how to hit a ball. I have seen him pray with his team, and I overheard one of the girls say, "Coach Paz you are such a great Christian example, I am so glad you are my coach." David also received his master's degree in math in 2006 at Texas Tech in Lubbock, Texas. In the 2009-10 school year, David was selected as coach of the year. David moved to Arizona, where he teaches math, pre-calculus, trigonometry, and algebra. He also is a girl's volleyball coach there. I believe that God had a plan for David's life and allowed him to live when the doctor did not think it was possible. David is on the mission committee at his local church, where they support two missionaries to Brazil. He also has taught the adult Bible class and other classes.

John's strong Christian example has flowed down to blossom and grow in his children, as is evident in their lives.

Chapter 10

Healing Methods That Help Bipolar Patients and All Humanity

The following are the methods we tried to help us cope with bipolar disorder:

Medications: lithium, trazadone, Lexapro, Depakote, Prozac, Inderal, Seroquel, risperidone, Lamictal, Zoloft, lorezepam, Ambien, Xanax, Abilify, Wellbutrin, Klonopin, Cymbalta, Ritalin, Luvox, Tegretol, Zyprexa, Buspar, gabapentin, Remeron, and Viibryd. John still takes Zyprexa and lorezepam.

Electric Shock: John had twenty-one shock treatments.

Vitamins and Supplements: Many vitamins and nutritional supplements are said to be helpful, such as the B vitamins, omega-3, mangosteen, astaxanthin, vitamin D3, magnesium, zinc, manganese, and selenium. Two powerful brain-enhancers are huperzine A, and vinpocetine. Stay away from aspartame, as this artificial sweetener adversely affects the brain.

Therapy: John had several therapists in two states, one analyst, and one psychotherapist. The psychotherapist got the closest to John's negative false core beliefs that were tormenting him.

Vagus Nerve Implant: This is the implant that goes to the vagus nerve.

Alternative Mind Methods:

- o   Hypnosis, Alan B. Densky
- o   Holosync, Bill Harris
- o   The Healing Codes, Alex Lloyd
- o   Emotion Codes, Bradley Nelson
- o   Manifesting Intelligence, Dr. Robert Anthony
- o   Learning Strategies, Paul Scheele and Win Wenger
- o   New Transformation Strategies, Kenji Kumara
- o   The Genius Code
- o   Brain Wave Entrainment (BWE)
- o   Prayer

John started the Healing Codes, which is a method that can change one's negative beliefs into a positive state of mind. This started to help John in several different areas of his life. He really responded to this method of healing and improved for about two months, but something happened, and he returned to his deep depression and anxiety. I believe what happened was that one day, I was working on the Internet, and he confessed to me that he was jealous of me because I could use the Internet and my smartphone and drive our car; all of which he had not been able to do since 2003. This awareness threw him into a deep depression again.

Additionally, when we moved to Oklahoma, he left his friends, and that made him feel all the more desolate. His mental state was so fragile. He was guarding his heart and couldn't face his fears of what was lurking deep in his subconscious, as he dreaded the pain that it would bring. He returned to being negative and tormented to his very soul. I've already mentioned John's resistance to hypnosis, all types of therapy, several great psychiatrists in three states, twenty-one electric shock treatments, six hospitalizations, the vagus nerve implant, vitamin supplementations, and psychotropic medicines over the excruciating years in the winter of his life. After he tried the Healing Codes and Emotion Codes, he couldn't bear trying any of the other alternative methods, but in my search for understanding our conscious and subconscious minds, I found and tried these other methods. I found them to be extraordinary for helping to be more aware consciously, to understand why we do the things we do, and the power of our thoughts.

A wise man once stated, "A positive intention makes a great direction." When you wake up in the morning, put a positive intention in your mind to assure the right direction in life. I have listened to many world-renowned, inspiring speakers and many creative, intelligent, spiritual, and incredible giants in my life through a lot of seminars, the Internet, traveling on three continents, and living eight years in Brazil. I would like to introduce some insights that I have acquired. I believe that my source for all this is from God, through His Word and having a close walk with my all-knowing, loving, creative, powerful Heavenly Father.

I hope I have inspired you to dream big dreams and believe that your Creator will bless you beyond your wildest imagination. The key here is, as Jesus stated, "Seek first the kingdom of God, and all these things will be added unto you" (Matthew 6:33, NIV).

I believe if you put God first in your life, then He will bless you with all the joys a person can hold, and you will be filled with eternal bliss.

I have had a lot of time to pursue information and increase my knowledge since I retired. Our minds and thoughts are more powerful than we realize. When observing mankind early in human history in Babylonia, God saw that mankind was planning to build a city and a tower that would reach to the heavens. "The Lord said, 'Behold they are one people, and they all have the same language. And this is what they began to do, and now nothing which they purpose to do will be impossible for them'" (Genesis 11:6). This is an example of the possibilities, whether positive or negative, that mankind can accomplish through thoughts. In this example, however, their tower, known as the Tower of Babel, was going to be a monument to their own greatness, rather than to God's, so He confused their language and scattered them over the face of the earth; thus, all the different languages appeared in our world. One can see where the negative thoughts and energies, in this case, show that nothing would be impossible for man to accomplish through the futile thoughts in his mind and heart. This shows the potentially powerful energy we have as human beings from our thoughts.

I have recently discovered astounding information from several different sources (listed above under "Alternative Mind Methods"). These methods have opened a new awareness in me regarding the energy of the universe and how everything, including our bodies, is energy. Negative and positive emotions, which are forms of energy, affect us down to the cells of our bodies, and the cure for so many diseases is now available to humanity. The next frontier is energy medicine, one of the most powerful cures for all types of illnesses.

Hypnosis

Dr. John A. Scott Sr., my analyst, stated, "Healing requires that we find those deep conflicts and resolve them so that life may rediscover its purpose." Each human being is incredibly important, and we can be a great influence on people when we can accept what is to be. If we resist certain situations in our lives, we suppress ourselves. We also need to undo or replace the negative programming of our emotions in the brain and heart. We can process our thoughts through brain wave therapy (explained later).

Hypnosis is a powerful tool. John did not respond to it; he would not let anyone see into his subconscious mind. He guarded it and was not receptive to the hypnotist's suggestions. It's interesting to note that John took a course on hypnosis while in graduate school in 1968. His professor was this hypnotist that we went to see in 1980. John also took a course in hypnosis at East Texas State University in 1981. He used some of these techniques in his therapy with his patients.

Recently, I listened to a CD from a hypnotist that I believe would help many people. This CD puts you in a very relaxed state and bypasses the conscious mind. You don't need pills, shots, or drugs to experience tranquility. The most powerful instrument in our reality is the mind. One of the most powerful tools of persuasion is hypnosis. Motivational speakers Crystal and Mark Hanson explain:

> Hypnosis is like a mind excavation that can uncover hidden negative emotions. It creates a new identity. There are three steps to root out these destructive emotions: 1. Self-honesty without judgment creating *awareness*. 2. Make a deliberate decision to pay attention to this awareness. This involves quantum

physics, which is the study of the behavior of matter and energy at the molecular, atomic, nuclear, and even smaller microscopic levels. 3. Begin a deliberate repetition to move toward what you really want. The subconscious mind holds the program for the past. It is a storage tank that contains what has happened when you were much younger, and thus we become encoded. Hypnosis can help excavate the depths of the unconscious mind, where false negative core beliefs reside. Hypnotherapy is a method of communicating with your unconscious mind to negotiate rapid and permanent changes.

As I've mentioned, I underwent hypnosis with an excellent analyst. It was incredible to look into my own subconscious mind and see the hurt and pain, as well as seeing something that was bothering me when I had no conscious awareness of the fact. It's believed that patients under hypnosis will not do anything against their will, but I found that to be false. My analyst asked me a question that I didn't want to answer in my awake state, but when I was hypnotized, I gave him the answer right away.

There are pros and cons to hypnotherapy, but ultimately, I received awareness and an understanding of why I had such a drive to be a missionary, as well as understanding why feelings from my childhood directed me to do what I did in my life. Hypnotist Alan B. Densky offers a program on CD in which the subconscious mind is programmed to make the listener feel peaceful and mellow. He believes in the power of mind over matter. Densky has an incredible, commanding voice that penetrates the subconscious mind with suggestions to help with anxiety and other negative emotions. He is the author of *Do-It-Yourself Hypnosis* and works with a neurolinguistic program.

Holosync

Bill Harris is the creator of Holosync Audio Technology, which creates the brain-wave patterns of meditation, along with many other beneficial states and instant mental abilities. This healing tool has been used by well over one million people in 193 countries. In 2003, Mr. Harris spoke at the United Nations regarding this healing method. The method of listening to mind-enhancing CDs can process our thoughts through brain-wave therapy. The listener can achieve complete relaxation, develop more creativity, and enjoy a serene calmness. Through these CDs, I have experienced this state of being, and it is truly incredible how this technology can improve life to the fullest. I require a lot less sleep, and tension melts away. New neural pathways are established in the brain, where our threshold of tolerance rises and stress does not overwhelm us as before. Most people realize that the left brain is where we find the analytical processing. The right brain contains the creative, inspirational, and intuitive abilities. I can attest to the fact that these CDs actually can synchronize the left and right brains. Einstein's brain was believed to be like this. I experienced purely right-brain functioning in my life before I started taking lithium, having an enormous amount of creativity and inspiration on the mission field in Brazil. I was able to rise around three o'clock in the morning and be so creative, making my Bible lessons for the children. I was so inspired for most of my life, and that lifted me to great heights. Eventually, I couldn't handle all the stress I encountered, so I experienced the devastating psychosis, the agony and the ecstasy of the bipolar mind.

The term *whole brain* means the left and right brains are synchronized, where one is able to release all the creativity and inspirational aspects of the right brain and have the intellect and analytical components of the left brain. We can then manifest awareness and the full potential that our Creator intended for all humanity. Awareness creates choice. When we are functioning on autopilot from the influence of the subconscious mind, things just happen to us. We are unaware consciously. When we become aware, our thoughts become a choice in our behavior. We need the knowledge of how our subconscious mind is programmed. How we feel is a choice, and how we behave is a choice also. This is something we do when we see something that triggers an emotion. This is a result of the symptom–producing event, usually in childhood. Many times, behavior is created outside our conscious awareness. If we observe ourselves, we can see why we do the things we do. Once we are more aware, we can make better choices of behavior and choose what serves us. This is called cognitive behavior, where we notice, pay attention, recognize, observe, and grasp.

How do you feel about the events in your life? What attitudes do you demonstrate to the positive and negative experiences you encounter? The way I understand this, it is the unconscious mind that adds all these meanings to our minds and has a huge influence in our lives. We all have this internal map of reality, which can be a helpful resource or non–resource. Early childhood experiences set patterns such as fear.

I have found that meditating with these CDs creates good feelings in my brain. When you focus on something, you get ideas, then resources come to your mind, and then you get motivated, persistent, and manifest courage. Conscious awareness is a key to the good life.

I believe these CDs alter brain-wave patterns, using both sides of the brain, which is described as the whole brain. According to Bill Harris, this new technology is called Centerpointe's Proprietary Autofonix Silent Communication technology. He explains that this creates new neural pathways in the brain. I can attest to that, after having listened to these CDs for several months. I believe listening to them improved my cognitive abilities and profoundly raised my threshold to better handle stress, which is so devastating to the body, mind, and spirit.

We should keep our minds on what we want and off what we don't want. The memories in our subconscious mind tend to manifest in our life. It's so intriguing to think that these CDs can build our brain muscles and that now brain waves can be measured by highly sensitive machines.

Most people try to change their bad habits with willpower. You don't have willpower; it's your conscious mind's intention to override your subconscious mind. For a while your "willpower" will work, but then you get distracted by people or situations in life, and then you go back to the old habits that you had. You have to reprogram your subconscious mind. According to Mr. Harris, you are using the wrong part of your brain, your conscious mind.

I bought three CDs from Bill Harris's Centerpointe program. With these CDs came a pamphlet that describes brain waves:

> Twenty-four hours a day, nerve cells in your brain communicate with each other. They generate electrical impulses that fluctuate rhythmically in distinct patterns called brain-wave patterns. There are four brain waves: Beta includes concentration, arousal, and alertness. Alpha is a state of relaxation,

super-learning, relaxed focus, meditation, and the beginning of access to the unconscious mind. When you learn to enhance your brain's natural alpha waves, a whole new world opens up because you are adding intuitive activity to your usual logical neural activity; you become more creative and aware. Theta brain wave is the pattern of increased creativity, visionary experiences, and a deeper meditation. Delta wave is a dreamless sleep, access to the unconscious mind, and deep loss of body awareness.

In his book *Thresholds of the Mind*, Bill Harris observes, "Scientists have also found that the endorphins released when the brain is exposed to alpha and theta binaural beat patterns enhance many mental functions. Endorphins have a powerful strengthening effect on learning and memory, for instance, and have been known to reverse amnesia." Bill Harris, *Thresholds of the Mind, Your Personal Roadmap to Success, Happiness, and Contentment* (Beaverton, OR: Centerpointe Press, 2007) page 169.

The first time I listened to the delta wave on a CD, I fell into the deepest sleep. It was such a satisfying experience. I have been able to reach all of these states. It is so amazing to go in the deepest delta brain wave. This can improve your health, vitality, and well-being; raise your stress threshold sky high; and improve your mental abilities, creativity, focus, and concentration. It can create incredible, lasting peace of mind. I believe that this method can reach the deepest levels of our brain waves. Einstein's brain was this way. He had brain synchronization, which is "whole brain thinking." These CDs lead to incredible mental abilities. It really has a tremendous reduction on overall stress levels. The release and falling away of dysfunctional mental and emotional patterns such as anger, fear, anxiety, depression, sadness, substance abuse, and self-limitations is a tremendous relief. I believe this has helped me in many ways. When I ordered these Holosync CDs, they came with a CD titled *Super-Longevity*. This is an extraordinary CD that takes the listener on a journey to the depths of the heart, cells, the endocrine system, and DNA. "This soundtrack uses the Holosync sound technology to induce a theta brain-wave state. The silent affirmations have been formulated using Centerpointe's proprietary Autofonix silent communication technology." It starts out with a commanding, authoritative male voice that gently carries you to picture or think of the deepest, strongest unconditional love and compassion. Then he directs you to move that to your heart, and with each beat of your heart, concentrate on that unconditional love and feel the vibration or the conscious frequency of love. Another concept of vibration in this area is the result of an increase in self-awareness as we realize that everything is energy, and we become familiar with and experience the energy fields of love. After a few times of listening to this CD, I did feel the vibration.

From there you would transfer that love to all your trillions of cells and feel them vibrate. From there you would transfer that overwhelming love to your chromosomes—that holds the code that is unique to you—and then to your DNA. He repeats over and over again, "You and your DNA are one, and now you can communicate with your DNA. You are activating your ability to heal yourself and function optimally at every level. You do all things, consciously and unconsciously, to extend and enhance the length and quality of your life. Your endocrine system is functioning perfectly to create the hormones your body needs to enhance the length and quality of your life."

I have had problems with my thyroid gland for several years. In 2009, I had a biopsy of my enlarged gland; it was not cancer. In 2011, my primary doctor thought I had an overactive thyroid gland. In March 2012, I had a lot of blood tests done. He referred me to an endocrinologist. That summer I went to see the specialist and had more extensive blood tests in July 2012. During this time, I was listening to this CD, along with another healing CD on improving one's health. I believe these CDs were healing my thyroid gland. When the most recent blood tests came back, they showed my thyroid gland was completely normal—no overactive thyroid! I had an ultrasound in August 2012, as the endocrinologist suspected I had an auto-immune problem. It showed I had multiple nodules on the right and left of my thyroid gland, so I had a biopsy in four locations of my thyroid; they were all benign. I believe that because I listened to those CDs repeatedly, it did influence my endocrine system. My blood tests showed, in addition to the normal thyroid levels, that I increased my "good" HDL cholesterol six points and lowered my diabetic numbers significantly to where my diabetes is being well controlled. My calcium and potassium levels returned to normal as well. That was incredible, as it had been only four months since the last blood tests.

After nine months, I lowered my triglycerides fifty-one points. My HDL levels increased by sixteen points. This made a believer out of me about the powerful effect of the mind on the body and the beneficial CDs that I listened to. Not only did my physical health improve, but my mental state was clearer. My emotional state is one of peace and joy; my life is so blessed. I was having a lot of insomnia, but after listening to all these CDs I am now sleeping like a baby. I highly recommend these CDs.

Learning Strategies Corporation

This company uses the Holosync technology in its CDs. Pete Bissonette, president of Learning Strategies Corporation, explains how Paul Scheele, cofounder of Learning Strategies, and Win Wenger, mind development pioneer, put together a program called *Genius Code*, pointing out that we are brighter, sharper, and smarter than we think we are. As they affirm:

> You have the capability to use your mind like Einstein, Edison, Galileo, and Da Vinci. All you need to do is tap into the part of your brain that is the ultra-intelligent professor. You will learn how to use your mind for your own creative problem solving. And how do you do that? With *Genius Code*, the breakthrough program that turns daydreams into big ideas and solutions. It's as simple as daydreaming … with a twist. *Genius Code* allows you to improve your performance in virtually all aspects of mental ability, including—but not limited to—memory, quickness, IQ, and learning capacity.
>
> Pete Bissonette, president of Learning Strategies,
> www.learningstrategies.com/BillCD

I have four CDs by Paul Scheele from the Learning Strategies Corporation. I can testify that these CDs have helped me tremendously in my mental and physical health, as well as learning how to carry on the appropriate discussion with an individual or speak in front of hundreds of people. I want to emphasize that knowledge is power, and we can be empowered to rise above to achieve all that we were made to be. Learning Strategies is located at 2000 Plymouth Road, Minnetonka, Minnesota 55305-2335. They can be reached at 1-866-292-1861. In an advertisement I received in the mail, Win Wenger states:

> Research shows that the exceptional achievements of famous thinkers are the result of mental conditioning. You can condition your own mind in the same way through a simple process called "image streaming." With image streaming, you tap into the unending flow of images and thoughts that flow from your mind. When you condition your brain, the world changes instantly and immediately. For years, scientists cited that one out of three Americans was unable to visualize. And—oh, yes—I was one of those who absolutely could not until I used these methods to get pictures for myself. … Since then, out of the thousands of people I have taught to image stream, every person has succeeded and thus enjoyed the benefits of visual thinking. You may be asking yourself, what else is my brain capable of doing? You will develop striking awareness that gives you insights and wisdom beyond what you could ever expect to have. Crack your personal Genius Code to make your life worthwhile and attain absolute self-confidence in all you do. The subconscious mind can process twenty thousand pieces of information at a time. The conscious mind—that

little voice in the back of your head—can only handle seven pieces of information at a time. That's why you can dial a friend and moments later forget whom you are calling. The conscious mind is limited. Tap the power of your mind to get raging courage, tenacity, and confidence for anything from deciding which day care is best for your child to buying a multibillion dollar company, from developing a skill to attaining great wealth, from achieving your goals to enjoying health and well-being. You name it.

Paul Scheele and Win Wenger also state:

What if you were brighter than you think? Have you ever told yourself that you cannot do, be, or have something? Why, then, can someone else enjoy more of life's abundance? Imagine the excitement of owning unlimited resources with a key to access them. Human development experts have shown that you possess resources enough to soar through life and make profound contributions in the world. If you have been conditioned to believe less of yourself, then you may have been missing a key factor. Think of it as your access code.

The *Genius Code* reveals the amazing but simple secrets for discovering your personal access code. Use these secrets to activate your capacities for genius. Although described in great writings throughout the ages, virtually no one has ever taught them in school.

This personal learning course will help you gain new tools for genius. In the true fashion of some of the world's greatest thinkers, you will learn to think broader and deeper and face challenges with new skills.

Genius Code is predicated on the notion that you are much brighter than you may think. You have an astounding neurological heritage within you and vast abilities that can be used to improve the quality of life for you, your family, friends, and community. It is our sincere desire that you "crack the code" on how to receive the gifts of your brain's genius. Start using your greater resources to enjoy the immediate and far-reaching benefits.

The Healing Codes

This is my favorite of the healing methods. The assessment test is incredible and is free to those who want to test themselves on their heart issues. This is found at thehealingcodes.com. It takes about ten minutes to do, and then there are twelve pages that explain the results that can be printed out. This shows approximately where you are in your development of the spiritual, mental, emotional, and physical health. This is based on the fruits of the Spirit as mentioned in Galatians 5:22-23 (NIV), which reads: "The fruit of the Spirit is love, joy, peace, patience, kindness, goodness, faithfulness, gentleness and self-control." The two authors of this book are Alexander Loyd, ND, PhD, and Ben Johnson, MD, DO, NMD. This concept is found in Proverbs 4:23. This is a three-thousand-year-old admonition. King Solomon, known to this day for his wisdom and his understanding of human nature, writes that a person should guard his heart above everything else, because it determines the course of your life. The NIV translation reads: "Above all else, guard your heart for it is the wellspring of life." We believe the heart is the seat of our unconscious or subconscious mind. Dr. Bruce Lipton, a Stanford biologist, may have been the first person to identify these spiritual heart issues from a scientific perspective. His work shows that over 90 percent of what affects our thoughts, feelings, and actions can be attributed to unconscious memories stored in our bodies. Southwestern Medical School calls them cellular memories. These memories contain wrong beliefs about ourselves, others, life, and God, and these wrong beliefs create physiological stress. These cellular memories are in cells all over the body. These negative memories, such as fear, anger, and guilt, go to the cells and flip on the stress switch in the hypothalamus. This stress suppresses the immune system, drains your energy, and causes you to fail. You have to go to the root source of the problem, which is cellular memory. The Healing Codes activate the destructive memories. According to the authors, there are four healing centers in the body. You activate them with energy from your fingertips, while repeating truth-focused positive statements that replace the negative destructive memories. This may be hard to understand until you try it and realize the power of this positive energy. You would need to get the book for a full explanation and guide to the Healing Codes. There are three things to remember, as Dr. Loyd emphasizes: It's not your fault; the solution is not trying harder; and you can still get to where you want to be.

With enough stress, over time, something physical is often the first thing to give, and health problems often result. Dr. Lipton goes on to say that if you can heal the wrong beliefs, even genetic illness and disease can be healed. A wrong belief is basically a lie about the true nature of reality, and we need to shine truth and light into our hearts to correct these lies. The authors also say that they realized that everything at its root is an energy frequency ($E=mc^2$) and that illness and disease can be traced to an unhealthy energy frequency. (This is precisely the way an MRI determines health problems.) They found that if you can change the unhealthy frequency to a healthy one, the illness or disease will go away without drugs, surgery, counseling, or even effort.

The Healing Codes use unseen energy to remove unknown and unseen things that may be causing harm to people. Those unknown and unseen things we call "pictures of the heart." The Healing Codes work because of established laws of nature from the field of quantum physics, laws that have been validated and accepted for at least seventy-five years. Quantum physics is a branch of science that deals with discrete, indivisible units of energy called quanta, as described by the quantum theory. It describes the nature of the universe as being much different from the world we see. Quantum physics has been able to go to the subatomic particles so far. Albert Einstein thought this energy had the appearance of being solid. Thomas Young, a noted physicist of that day, believed that energy existed as a wave form and not particles at all. They both agreed that *all* things were comprised of energy. Einstein's theory of relativity breaks down from the infinitely large to the infinitely small for example: cosmos - universe - galaxy - earth - individuals - organ systems - cells - molecules - atoms - subatomic particles = energy (light). We do not see things as they are; we see things as we are!

What is so interesting is that a brilliant scientist, Niels Bohr, believed that energy could be both waves and particles. It was discovered later, as technology advanced, that these waves/particles *did* consist of waves that behaved and turned into particles. This point is crucial to understanding how our thoughts create our own reality. This energy took form immediately, based on the *thoughts* and *beliefs* of the scientist who was observing it. When a scientist studied this energy with the expectation (thought or belief) of seeing particles, as Einstein did, particles were observed. If another scientist studied them with the expectation of seeing waves, waves are what he saw. A simple analogy of this is when an optimist sees a partially filled glass of milk, he says the glass is half full. When a pessimist looks at the glass, he says the glass is half empty. The glass of milk did not change, but two different people saw the same object differently, based on their thoughts, beliefs, and emotions. Another way of looking at this is the phrase, "Beauty is in the eye of the beholder." One person can look at another person and say, "that is the ugliest person I have ever seen." Someone else will look at that same person and say, "There is so much character within that person so that all that is seen is the inward beauty."

"The conclusion then was that this energy, these subatomic particles *acted* and *responded* in exact proportion to the 'thoughts' and 'beliefs' that the scientist who was studying them had at that moment. Our thoughts are also creative. We are all creators of our reality. Our thoughts are energy. Thoughts are determined by our beliefs, which form our perceptions." We have the ability to mold and shape the various areas of our lives, based on how we choose to think, believe, and feel!" abundance-and-happiness.com. This is how quantum physics explains how our thoughts are energy.

Theoretical physicist Max Planck said, "Scientists cannot solve the ultimate mystery of nature, and that is because, in the last analysis, we ourselves are a part of the mystery that we are trying to solve." Through much study, I believe spiritual wisdom from God has been conveyed in spiritual circles for thousands of years, and the recent discoveries made through quantum physics pertaining to our creative ability are consciously and intentionally molding and shaping our reality. The spiritual wisdom and direction that has been provided can awaken, enlighten, and empower us to the real truth concerning our infinite and limitless capabilities. We need to renew our minds, "and do not be conformed to the world, but be transformed by the renewing of your mind, that you may prove what is that good and acceptable will of God" (Romans 12:2, NKJV). "Now faith is the substance of things hoped for, the evidence of things not seen" (Hebrews 11:1, NKJV). Jesus said, "If you believe, you will receive whatever you ask for in prayer" (Matthew 21:22, NIV). This, of course, is if it is according to His will. As you believe, so shall you receive.

The Healing Codes allow us to heal the body in a way we have never done before, because we discover new ways to use quantum physics. With the Healing Codes, we take steps to deliver positive and loving energy to the body for it to use in healing itself. The Healing Codes make bio-energy available to us, using a new but natural delivery system. In short, the Healing Codes activate a physical function built into the body by God that consistently and predictably removes the number-one cause of illness and disease from the body—stress. Proverbs 14:30 says, "A heart at peace gives life to the body, but envy rots the bones" (NIV). This is another key point to remember: God designed our bodies to maintain optimal health. Stress kills, and wrong beliefs cause stress. Ninety percent of the time, the source of a problem is unconscious. The self-protection mechanisms in the body resist being healed. This is amazing healing energy. The authors of the Healing Codes believe that the energy frequency of pure love will heal anything—and that it may be the only power that will. The vibrational or conscious frequency of love is the ultimate healing resource. "Love is a universal vibration; love communicates to all species, functions on all levels and expresses our true nature. It is the foundation of all healing and the core essence of the life-force." Richard Gordon, Quantum-Touch, the Power to Heal, Berkeley, North Atlantic Books, 2006, page 26. Dr. Andrew Weil believes "all illness is psychosomatic. It's not physical at its origin." I really believe this method is a profound and powerful means to wellness.

Emotion Codes and Body Codes

This method is by Dr. Bradley Nelson. This is similar to the Healing Codes but takes a different approach to arrive at the same results. Dr. Nelson also recognizes God and prayer as the ultimate solution to our problems. I bought six DVDs that explain this technique. It is another profound method of healing. From a DVD I bought on the Emotion Codes, Dr. Nelson states:

> Just as the effects of the wind are felt rather than seen, trapped emotions are invisible, yet can exert a powerful influence upon you. ... It is my experience that a significant percentage of physical illness, emotional difficulty, and self-sabotage are actually caused by these unseen energies. ... Trapped emotions can create depression, anxiety, and other unwanted feelings that you can't seem to shake. Mankind needs to live on a higher consciousness. There is infinite potential when the Divine (God) flows through you. We can then be abundantly blessed, joyful, and authentic.

We just manifest everything positive, like breathing in life and love. As stated, all we have or possess is the present. Remember the brevity of life. We must speak truthfully, act creatively, and be authentic. Our confidence will rise when we help others and thus our purpose will be evident. Once we know who we are, as well as knowing our purpose here on Planet Earth, then there is nothing that can hinder us in achieving all that our Creator intended for us to be. It can be an incredible life! We will have power backed by love; everything will manifest in your life like joy, peace and contentment.

Dr. Nelson shows how to release your trapped emotions for abundant health, love, and happiness. In trying to help each of his patients, he always says a prayer to God before he assists in this healing process. This impressed me. This method involves muscle testing to communicate with the subconscious mind, much like a lie detector test shows whether a person is telling the truth or not. We have a physical response when we tell the truth or tell a lie. This involves the subconscious mind. We can actually communicate with our subconscious minds. The muscles are instantly weakened when we lie. They stay strong when we tell the truth. This method can free trapped negative and false emotions. Mankind is just now beginning to understand the mysterious nature of energy, how it works, and how it can be harnessed. I am fascinated with quantum physics.

According to Dr. Nelson, scientists have learned that all of the tissue and organs in the body produce specific magnetic vibration. They call them biomagnetic fields. Everything that exists radiates vibrational energy that has an ultimate effect on our own energy field, whether good or bad. Everything is energy. On a website, Christie Marie Sheldon of "Love or Above" asks the question:

How can you manifest without the right vibration? The energy that runs through everything on the whole planet can be measured. All things have a personal energetic frequency, including you. Your personal energetic frequency determines what your life looks like and how successfully you navigate through life. In his book *Power vs. Force*, Dr. David Hawkins illustrated a chart that is called the scale of consciousness. For example, the energetic value of shame is 20, which means "I am not enough." Guilt is 30, meaning "I am bad." Hate is 50, grief is 75, fear is 100, courage is 200, joy is 540, peace is 600, and enlightenment is 700. The average energetic value on the planet is 207. Adolf Hitler was 45, Mother Teresa was 700.

[Japanese author and entrepreneur] Dr. Emoto proved that higher energetic frequencies like gratitude, thanks, and appreciation can influence objects like water into higher and lower energetic frequencies. Dr. William Braud at the Mind Science Foundation conducted research that proves a person can change and affect how long a red blood cell will last. Embodying the energy at the highest level possible is what creates a successful life. In life, events happen that can affect your frequency. Growing up, we all have ... events and trauma. All the thoughts, beliefs, and ideas you

receive from your family were either from the higher
self or lower self.

We are beings of energy, and there is an intelligent force at work
in the universe (God). Dr. Nelson states that unresolved traumatic
events live in the energy system of the body and cause blockages
in the energy flow. For centuries, the Chinese have known about
this energy field, qi, and they are able to free this energy through
acupuncture and other ancient methods.

Manifestation Intelligence

This is a set of 101 powerful affirmations that are designed to help
you rewire your subconscious mind and more easily achieve your
goals, much like the Healing Codes. Jeremiah 10:23 (NKJV) says: "It
is not in man who walks to direct his own steps." Our Creator made
us and knows what we need. Dr. Robert Anthony, a hypnotherapist
from Manifestation Intelligence, notes that the secret of deliberate
creative state occurs on two levels:

1. Alignment with the laws of quantum physics. Thoughts,
   positive or negative, attract their equivalent or vibrational
   match. For example: think good thoughts, attract good
   things; think bad, negative, or needy thoughts, and you'll
   attract bad and negative things in your life. Emotion is a key.
   Most of us send out far stronger emotional signals about the
   things we don't want than those we do want.
2. Conscious and subconscious alignment. Your conscious
   desires and your subconscious intention must be in
   alignment. If your conscious mind wants one thing and

your subconscious mind wants something else (counter-intention), it is impossible to create what you truly want. Sure, you can temporarily trick yourself into getting something while you are out of alignment, but in the end, it never lasts. Science is teaching us more and more every day about the relationship between the conscious and the subconscious minds. This is a tidal wave of new information. I did not read all 101 affirmations, but I believe that is a good, positive thing to do.

According to Dr. Anthony, hypnosis is the fastest way to change the subconscious. You have to allow the subconscious mind time to change, to allow it to do its thing. Self-hypnosis is a great method. You can access this information in books and on the Internet. You can re-pattern the subconscious mind through self-hypnosis. Hypnosis is a state of being, a narrow focusing on something as a filter. We're always in a trance of some kind. For example, you are driving down the street and thinking intensely about something, while not realizing where you just were, as if you are on autopilot. You were in a type of a trance. You just have to change the negative trance. We can de-hypnotize the old trance.

Dr. Anthony says mind viruses are programmed in childhood by parents, authority figures, and others. When a child is told by authority figures that, for instance, he is bad or stupid, this is downloaded as a fact into the child's subconscious mind. These false beliefs rob us as we react to life, based on our false negative core beliefs. We act in habitual beliefs.

When I was little, my mother told me if I didn't quit some bad behavior that she would "half kill" me. My young mind pictured me, half dead. It is hilarious now, but then it was a nightmare for my sensitive and impressionable psyche. It was effective, as I stopped whatever I was doing. More counselors, psychologists, and therapists are finding the source that causes most all disease—stress! Hidden deep in the subconscious mind are so many false beliefs that a child acquires, and this creates such stress on the rest of one's life. It has shown to adversely affect us emotionally, spiritually, and physically. At my graduation from high school, my father indicated that I would not amount to anything (even though I was on the honor roll my junior and senior year). This devastated me, because I was always a good girl (due to the fact that my subconscious mind was programmed that if I disobeyed, my mother would half kill me).

Dr. Robert Anthony emphasizes that we can change our subconscious blueprint. We actually have two brains: the conscious and the subconscious. The conscious mind is the everyday state of awareness. It is good at planning things and planning for the future. It allows us to have self-awareness and to appreciate the good things in life. Reasoning and logic rest in the conscious mind in the left brain, and our creative, inspirational, and intuitive states reside in the right brain. The subconscious mind controls insight and wisdom. It is our connection to a higher authority; to me, this means God, our Creator. Positive and negative experiences influence our conscious minds. The subconscious mind holds the emotions that fuel and drive our conscious thinking. This, I believe, is what happened to John, as he believed a lie when he was told at the age of ten that he was going to hell. The subconscious mind stores memories and information for when we need it. We operate mostly automatically, as if we're on autopilot from our subconscious minds, and so the conscious mind is limited. Children develop core beliefs in the state of the hypnotic trance. The subconscious mind is in charge of our habits. It resists change and likes routine and putting forth the least effort. John has been resistant to all attempts to be healed. I understand that millions of people around the world have been cured because of the healing methods I describe here from all the great speakers I have heard.

The Now Method

This method is a form of mental discipline that can transform a person's life. This is a system of understanding the causes of depression. I believe Jesus' words, "So do not worry about tomorrow, for tomorrow will care for itself. Each day has enough trouble of its own" (Matthew 6:34, NASV). In Isaiah 43:18, God states, "Do not call to mind the former things, or ponder things of the past" (NASV). Paul said in Philippians 3:13, "One thing I do: Forgetting what is behind and straining toward what is ahead. I press on toward the goal to win the prize for which God has called me heavenward in Christ Jesus" (NIV).

If we can put the past in the past and not worry or fret about the future, then we can have peace and contentment that can create a powerful energy for the "now." We will be released from all the negativity we have experienced in life. This negativity holds us back from setting our spirits free to dream, hope, and accomplish goals and aspirations that have been hidden away in our subconscious minds. When we do not dwell on what we are going to do about future problems and challenges, we are again set free to be all we were created to be in the "now." Anyone can achieve this with a little practice.

I recently attained this state of being after wasting so much time and energy with my feelings of apprehension aimed at the future and the negative core beliefs of the past. This has drained so much energy that could have been more wisely used in the present—the "now." Yes, we need to plan for the future, but so many times our plans take wings and fly in another direction. It is clear by now how I feel about the providence of God in our lives. There is an indescribable peace in knowing that our Creator knows what is best for us, day by day; it takes faith to believe the future is in God's hands. In some ways, this concept is new to me after all these years of habitually dwelling on the past and the future. This is futile thinking. We can't change the past, but we can let it go. What we do in the "now" can give us a glorious and rewarding future. Our negative and positive thoughts are so powerful that they can change our lives for the better or the worse. Again, the profound words of the Bible in Proverbs 23:7: "As he thinks in his heart, so is he" (NKJV). Are our thoughts hopeful and full of great expectations for our lives, or are they apprehensive, fretting over what dread could be facing us in the future? We sometimes are blinded to the tremendous amount of energy in these thinking patterns. The apostle Paul admonishes mankind to hope "that the eyes of your heart may be enlightened" (Ephesians 1:18, NIV).

Life is a joy, now that I have let go of the past, and I don't have to fret over the future, such as whether I have enough money to make it through retirement or wondering what will happen if I get disabled or old and ugly. I am free of all the future and just reside in the present. I am all that I was meant to be in the "now." This empowerment can be for everyone. It only takes self-discipline to stay focused on the "now," thereby releasing all the negative worrying and freeing your mind to soar with creativity and the excitement of life in the present. My husband used to say, "Worrying is just shoveling smoke." Living in the "now" is a process that releases negative emotions, frees people from the past, and relieves anxiety about the future. This gives us empowerment, and ideas will pop into our conscious minds as we are more of an intuitive person. This journey awakens our minds and spirit. As best-selling self-development author Sonia Ricotti has said, "Just trust that everything is unfolding the way it is supposed to. Don't resist. Surrender to what is, let go of what was, and have faith in what will be. Great things are waiting for you around the corner."

New Transformation Strategies

This is transformation in the quantum by Kenji Kumara. He also mentions the concept of quantum physics. Many self-help people and world-renowned speakers endorse these methods. I am fascinated with these types of healing methods and will continue my search for knowledge, wisdom, and understanding. The brain goes into the theta and delta brain waves in this strategy. This state of vibration (consciousness) and perception can be taught. To do this, one has to use the force of unconditional love and allowance. This is the essential vibration. Any kind of doubt and fear won't work. This vibration can work. According to Mr. Kumara, we all have a vibration. We need to get our act together to solve our difficulties and to learn to be peacemakers. He also encourages mankind to get to the place of oneness, working in the "now" moment. Thought and consciousness is a vessel by which minds can communicate; this communication is happening all the time. Thoughts inspire. It's good to imagine what you want to manifest in your life. Albert Einstein said, "Imagination is a preview of life's coming attraction. Without imagination playing in your mind, the manifestation will not occur. Imagination = inspiration = manifestation." I believe Einstein had an abundance of imagination in his life like little children have and then they get stifled in later years resulting in their dreams being lost. We need to imagine and visualize using all our potential and possibilities that will carry us to soar to the heights of our Creator's vision for each of us.

My brother, Jake, is a genius. My father also told him he wouldn't be a success. That was all Jake needed to aspire to be great, in spite of what our father said. He did his PhD work at Kent State University, Kent, Ohio, in comparative animal physiology, with minors in cellular biology and molecular genetics. He was a college professor of anatomy and physiology. Even at the age of six, he had a lot of common sense and always told me, "You don't have any common sense!" I believed him and that thought went down to my subconscious mind as a fact and as part of my map of reality. I'm afraid I have lacked common sense all my life, but the other day, I did something that took common sense, and I was so proud of myself. I am improving in the area of common sense and am strengthening that weakness that I have had all my life, due in part to my genius brother convincing me that I had no common sense. I looked up to my big brother and believed what he said was true. When parents tell their kids that they are "bad" instead of saying, "You did a bad thing," the child downloads that he/she is bad.

Dr. Symeon Rodger of New Transformation Strategies titles his seminar "Transform Your Consciousness and Manifest the Life You Desire by Working through Your Body." According to Dr. Rodger, people get exactly the kind of life that they expect to get. He also stresses that you can change the subconscious mind. The idea of transforming your unconscious mind through your body is a new concept for many thinkers in today's world. Ancient scientists knew so much about consciousness. We are a mind/body entity, and the thinking patterns are deeply rooted in our subconscious minds. This thinking goes along with Dr. Bradley Nelson's "Body Codes."

Dr. Rodger believes that our emotional condition depends on the condition of our physical body. I questioned that conclusion, but he says, "Emotions are not in your head—they go much deeper. Intelligence is not localized in the brain. It is distributed in all parts of the body such as the gut. An example of this is the idea that you have butterflies in your stomach at times when certain situations arise. The false belief is that you are your brain, not your thoughts or emotions."

Esperanza Universal is another great webinar speaker from the New Transformation Strategies. She spoke on "Shift Your Consciousness; Experience Your Limitless Potential." She points out that we need to be aware of our feelings. We need to have pure feelings. Is it fear, anger, or some other negative emotion that controls you? She states that we should trace the feelings we have that stem from a belief long ago (the symptom-producing event). We trace it to the original event that caused this feeling, realizing the past belief is not the true us. We then need to make a conscious choice, affirming that we are love, joy, and peace. We need to bring belief to a higher vibration. People get stuck in their false beliefs.

Esperanza Universal also teaches about the potential we have in ourselves. You need to say, "I am loveable," and you have to be able to receive and give love. There is a law of reflection—what you see on the outside is also what you see on the inside. Choose to create your experiences. You will attract what you want. It is a higher vibration or consciousness of love. We need to stay in the present where we can have that love, joy, and peace by not worrying about the future. So many times, we live in our head and forget the heart. The heart has to lead. It connects to God. Your heart will tell you how you feel.

There are always spiritual laws that govern your life, and you should be in harmony with these laws. You are creating consciousness and not the subconscious. Remember who you really are. You must be in harmony with yourself. You are equal to everybody. *You are an ordinary person living an extraordinary life.* You need to know and to love yourself.

Remember, when you ask God for something, your prayers are answered. Ask God in a spirit of wholeness. Jesus said, "Ask and it will be given to you; seek and you will find; knock and the door will be opened to you. For everyone who asks receives; he who seeks finds; and to him who knocks, the door will be opened" (Matthew 7:7-8, NIV). God already knows what you are going to ask for. This is the law of expectation. We eagerly await the answer. The outcome is God, so let go of anxious thoughts. Above all, have gratitude and appreciation, and keep giving to others. In Jeremiah 29:11-12, God says, "For I know the thoughts that I think toward you, says the Lord, thoughts of peace and not evil, to give you a future and a hope" (NKJV).

I believe there is a lot of good from all these methods, but I also believe that the Bible is the manual of life. There is a treasure to be found within those pages.

Brain Wave Entrainment

I have several Brain Wave Entrainment MP3s from Super Mind Music. Thoughts inspire. They cause brain-wave frequencies. This is a fairly new field of understanding, so each person may want to do his/her own research and come to his/her own conclusion. I merely mention this to show what modern neuroscientists are finding out about brain waves. These MP3s are so powerful that you have to be eighteen years old or older and not listen to them longer than two hours a day. They cause brain waves to help synchronize the left and right brains.

Prayer

This, to me, is the most powerful method of healing, more so than all the above methods. I have developed a very close relationship with God because of so many trials, not only in the last ten years but when I went to a foreign country, learned a new language, was exposed to a new culture, was a new parent, and so many other challenges in my life. I have been able to climb many mountains as a result of depending on my Creator and seeking the most rewarding relationship a human can have. This involved my communication with Him (prayer) and His relationship with me (hearing His word from the Bible). I also believe when we seek Him with all our heart, we will find Him, as noted in Jeremiah 29:13-14 (NIV), the Lord said: "You will seek me and find me when you seek me with all your heart. I will be found by you." In the Psalms in the Old Testament, David pours his heart out to God, and God hears his praise as well as his agony. When we pray, we should have the mind-set of sincerity, humility, fervency, persistency, watchfulness, godly living, and self-denial in the name of Christ and with faith.

I have seen the answers to prayer in my life so many times, such as when I was thirteen and begged God to let me be a missionary. He then directed my life all those years until I was twenty-five years old and that prayer was answered. I remember also my fervent prayer for my baby boy to live, when even the doctor thought he would die. Whatever situation we find in our lives, we have this lifeline of prayer to the one who made us and knows what we need. God always answers our prayers; sometimes the answer is yes, sometimes no, and sometimes wait. I don't have anxiety in my life because I turn problems over to Him. I encourage everyone to learn to talk with God as a friend, shepherd, creator, comforter, guide, protector, Sovereign Lord, God Almighty, the Great I AM, the great healer, my Savior, and our Father. Life with God is the most rewarding, exciting, peaceful, inspiring, and love-filled existence in the universe, with the anticipation of heaven when this physical dwelling goes back to dust. Get to know Him. The meaning of "to know" is "to experience." This is the state of spiritual intercourse, a deep oneness with our Creator.

I have given an overview of several methods and concepts that have helped me and millions of people around the world as a result of God's direction and these world-renowned speakers. Holistic healing allows one to look on the inside at the heart and subconscious mind. At times, you create your own illusion, not your own reality. I believe that using psychiatric tools along with these methods could help many suffering people. We need to increase our awareness. The more aware we are of our subconscious mind, the more we can make the right choices. We must get rid of the limiting beliefs that inhibit our creativity and inspiration. I put a lot of emphasis on God's Word, the Bible, as I believe it has all the answers to man's problems, and it is the standard by which I measure all these healing methods. It is a treasure, and one has to dig and search to find all the wisdom, knowledge, and understanding that are abundantly there; then the answers will come. There were several speakers I listened to on the webinars with whom I disagreed, so be careful what you believe, and challenge every speaker and writer, including me. Remember when people really believed the earth was flat? The person who said that could have been a dynamic, charismatic and motivational speaker! A little knowledge can be a dangerous thing. The only book I wholeheartedly recommend without any reservation is THE BIBLE!

All these methods can be found on the Internet and in many books that I have read. I have found an enormous amount of useful information that has been a tremendous help in my life. These are not the mainstream cures but are powerful alternative methods that have helped so many people. As you have seen, many of these inspirational speakers and writers have some of the same theories, especially regarding the conscious and subconscious mind. I have several of the CDs with healing music, and it will send you into a new dimension of peace and creativity while your mind goes into the alpha and theta brain waves. Also, the paraliminal goes to the subconscious mind.—"Para" comes from the Greek and means "beyond," and "liminal" is Greek for "threshold." Thus, paraliminal means "beyond the threshold of conscious awareness." This is not the same thing as subliminal messages. These CDs from Paul Scheele of Learning Strategies are incredible to listen to. I believe they reach the subconscious mind through the music and the dynamic panoramic 3-D audio stereo technology. At times there are two speakers, one speaking in each ear at the same time. This is not as confusing as it sounds, because the subconscious mind can easily take in both speakers simultaneously. I listen to the right ear first and then, when I listen to the CD another time, I listen to the voice in the left ear.

The Current Response to John's Depression

I try to show unconditional love to John, to the extent that I can, and make allowances for his depression. However, at times I must show tough love to get him to see how his attitudes and "stinking thinking" cause him so much pain. At times, he suffers from self-pity.

I finally realized it was not up to me to heal John; that is between him and God. This is a daunting challenge for me, as I have to love him as he is and to make allowances for all the difficult behaviors he portrays. This takes an enormous amount of patience, perseverance, and determination on my part, but I believe the rewards will come. I am trying to build his self-confidence, self-esteem, and self-image and to help him wipe out all the fear, guilt, and dread in his life.

As this book goes to press, there has been very exciting news: two doctors accidentally found a medication to cure depression with no side effects. Many studies were conducted, and one formerly depressed man was interviewed. He said that this medication helped him quickly, and there were no side effects. However, it may take the FDA several years to approve it. This exciting news gives hope for relief from this tormenting state of being. Even though I feel that John's root cause of depression is unresolved, negative, false core beliefs, this recently found cure may be what helps him recover. As long as there is life, there is hope.

Chapter 11
Conclusion

Many people will challenge, criticize, and doubt these methods, but I hope everyone will have an open mind about the results of these eye-opening methods of awareness on the capabilities of the human mind. I like this statement from Lao Tzu: "The key to growth is the introduction of higher dimensions of consciousness into our awareness." Some people won't understand these concepts, as they do not have this knowledge and will think these ideas are absurd. I realize this, but I would urge everyone to reach for knowledge and understanding and "taste" the sweet results of becoming all we were created to be; to not miss out on the great adventure of life. Reject your self-limiting and self-sabotaging negative behavior. I believe that all human beings throughout the ages have lived on different levels, whether you identify it as higher/lower consciousness, higher/lower vibration, or brain-wave states of being.

I originally planned to finish this book when John achieved complete healing of his mind and spirit, but it appears it could take several years or death to resolve his bipolar depressive illness if he doesn't respond to these healing methods. I can't see the whole picture of John's situation. At times, it appears quite obvious that he has all these negative, trapped emotions, and what he needs to do is have faith and believe in one or several of these methods of healing. At other times, his illness appears to be a chemical imbalance in his brain, so maybe it will take time for his healing, or maybe this new cure for depression will help him. I have mentally and emotionally prepared myself for whatever happens, and I can face the worst-case scenario, because God is right with me, holding my right hand. What peace, joy, and comfort this affords.

Some people who suffer from bipolar disorder live their lives successfully without medication and doctors. One example is John's father. When he suffered his mania, he was the life of the party, on top of the world, and was very productive. Everybody loved him. When his father was in the depths of despair, he was extremely withdrawn, depressed, and quietly suffered the agony and torment of this disorder, yet he did not take any medication or see a psychiatrist for his condition. He was able to manage his life and to control his bipolar disorder in a socially acceptable way. My father suffered, as he was chained to the floor for ten months and beaten at times. He did have a doctor and stayed in an asylum. After about a year later, he regained his mental health and went on to live life to the fullest. He died at the age of ninety-one without ever taking medication for his illness.

There could be a combination of events, such as environment and heredity, at the core of John's bipolar disorder. No man is an island. We all have a rippling effect in our world. Each human is a unique being, and as Max Lucado states, "Your life has a plot; your years have a theme. You can do something in a manner that no one else can." What a world this would be if everyone knew what his or her purpose in life was meant to be and used that potential.

I do not know what John's outcome will be, but I do not have the time to wait for the answer. John is very healthy, physically, and could very well outlive me. Every bipolar individual reacts to this illness in his/her own way. I believe that in the near future, mankind will have more answers and solutions than we have today. I firmly believe that such methods as the Healing Codes, the Emotion Codes, and others are a tremendous source of treating this disorder, as well as many other illnesses of the body, mind, and heart. The Healing Codes did help John for a few months, but he was just too fragile emotionally to continue rising above. I give God all the glory and praise for allowing me to write our story.

The song "I Am a Promise" by Bill and Gloria Gaither includes the following lyrics:

> I am a promise, I am a possibility,
> I am a promise with a capital P,
> I am a great big bundle of potentiality.
> If I listen, I'll hear God's voice
> And if I am trying, He'll help me make the right choice.
> I am a promise, I see, with a great big capital P.

Do you see these three dynamic words—promise, possibility, and potentiality? With these concepts, you can blossom and become all you were made to be. I sang this song many times to children in the hope they would be aware of their own possibilities and potentiality by helping their subconscious minds to believe in themselves and to be a success in life.

When I was young, I used to read many books, like the condensed *Reader's Digest* books about American Indians, Greek mythology, and *National Geographic*. One day, I stood in my room and said, "Someday I'm going to write a book!" It was a childhood dream that I pursued and fulfilled. Many experiences, both the mountaintops and the valleys below, have enriched my life and stirred within my soul the burning desire to fulfill this dream and to inspire my fellow man. It only took a half century to accomplish this.

I would like to inspire and encourage young people to dream big dreams and believe that their Creator can take them by their right hand and lead them to achieve all their potential and possibilities. Isaiah 41:13 (NIV): "For I am the Lord, your God, who takes hold of your right hand and says to you, 'Do not fear; I will help you.'"

I have been exposed to many different cultures and have been given many opportunities to observe unique ways of thinking. At this point in my life I have a tremendous amount of peace, joy, love, and contentment. My threshold of stress is no longer overwhelming. I have reprogrammed my subconscious mind and enlightened the eyes of my heart. I am empowered to rise above the everyday anxieties of life. My physical, mental, emotional, and spiritual health is at an all-time high. This insight, which comes from the Lord, has elevated my life, and I want to inspire humanity to achieve all the potential that lies within each person.

Our subconscious minds gather information each day, far more than our conscious mind, and it tries to control and influence the conscious mind. During John's treatment with the great Dr. Angelo D. Christian, I wrote a letter to him, and I wanted to end the letter with an inspiring phrase about dreaming big dreams. I asked him to come "soar with me on the wings of a dream!" This phrase came to me from my subconscious mind. A few months after I wrote that in the letter, I was listening to a John Denver CD, and at the end of one of his songs, he sang that phrase. I have listened to this CD many, many times and never consciously remembered that phrase, but my subconscious caught that, and I was able to ascertain this information when I needed it. However, I later listened to the song, and what John Denver actually sang was, "Fly with me on the wings of a dream." I guess my subconscious mind liked "soar" better than "fly."

It has been a fascinating journey, and I encourage truth-seekers to know themselves and "soar with me on the wings of a dream." Realize and believe: "It is no secret what God can do. What He's done for others, He'll do for you!"

A very profound incident happened just before this book went to publication. In March 2013, John was sitting in my recliner in my office and I noticed his look of despair. I gently asked him: "You really suffered when you were a child didn't you?" He had big tears in his eyes and said: "Yes, I really suffered when I was a child!" He then left the room. John was brutally abused mentality, emotionally and spiritually when he was a child by adult authority figures. I shudder to think about how John was devastated as a child fearing eternal punishment. Later he returned to my office and cried out: "I'm going to cut my chest open so you can see my broken heart!"

In the past, John had closed his heart and guarded it so that no one and no treatment would penetrate where he has been hurting all these decades; not until that day when he opened his suffering heart to me. Finally he faced the truth about himself. His subconscious mind released all that hurt, anger, fear, guilt, despair, anxiety and depression. He was finally set free!

Appendix
Overview of the Life of Dr. John L. Paz

- John was born in Greenbrier, West Virginia, July 10, 1946.

- He received his BA at Barker Christian University in 1968. During John's years at Barker, he would drive three hours one way to a country congregation outside Little Rock, Arkansas, and preach on Sunday nights. He had so much drive and energy that he could manage all this activity. He received his master's degree in counseling in 1971 from Barker Graduate School of Religion. He obtained his doctorate degree in Ministry in 1991 from Fort Worth Christian University. He also studied human sexuality and hypnosis at East Texas State University in 1980. He attended the University of Nashville, studying cultural anthropology and Spanish. He attended PUCC University in Sao Paulo, Brazil, in the 1970s, studying psychopharmacology (a course on the effects of drugs on the brain). John studied at six universities on two continents.

- John and his wife, Joy, were missionaries in Brazil for eight years. They, along with three other couples, established a church in Sao Paulo, Brazil, and a church in Campinas, Brazil.

- John was instrumental in arranging for Wilson Children's Home to sponsor the children's home in the state of Sao Paulo, Brazil.

- John was the assistant director at the Christian camp in Sao Paulo, Brazil, working with the young people in the 1970s.

- John taught counseling to men at the Institute in Sao Paulo, Brazil, for training preachers and leaders for the Brazilian churches.

- Over the years, John and Joy made several trips to Brazil after returning to the States in 1980. One trip that John made was in the early '80s, when John recruited a team of college students to go on a campaign. Another trip was in 1997. John and Joy traveled with two board members of the children's home to assess the feasibility of sponsoring the children's home in Brazil. The third trip in 2002 was to help with a vacation Bible school. Joy went with a group in 2005 to help with a vacation Bible school and translated for the group.

- Upon his return to the States, John worked at Terrill Children's Home in Greenville, Texas, as a director of intake in 1980–1982. He then transferred to Porter Christian Children's Home in Oklahoma City and served thirteen years as the executive director.

- Dr. John Paz was an honored professional in the National Directory of Who's Who in Executives and Professionals.

- In June 1995, Dr. Paz accepted the position of Executive Director of Wilson Children's Home in Memphis, Tennessee. He served nine years as the director, as well as serving nine years as a leader for the church in Memphis.

- Starting in 1994, John started making humanitarian/ mission trips to Belarus (part of the former Soviet Union). He contacted an orphanage while there and explored the possibility of someday working toward the adoption process for couples in the States. John made a total of nine such trips to Belarus. He delivered medicines for the children's diabetic society and hospital supplies for the doctors there.

- John built a home at the farm for the children, as well as improving other areas of the campus at Wilson Children's Home. The community appreciated all these improvements, as the home had been rundown and was an eyesore to the city prior to John's leadership.

- John, with the board of director's approval, gave land for the Senior Citizens Center that was built. He was a board member of this organization. He loaned land for the Manzano High School Athletics to make a soccer field and a softball field.

- He gave land to build a barn for the therapeutic horse program.

- He spent an enormous amount of time and energy helping seven Albanians to attend the two-year college and later to graduate from the private Christian universities. John was able to convince the board of directors to pay for all the expenses for these Albanian students, which cost over two hundred thousand dollars.

- He was a member of the Kiwanis Club of Memphis and served as one of the presidents. He was awarded the Tablet of Honor for Services to Children of the World. He has touched the lives of children in Brazil, Albania, Russia, and the United States.

- The former governor of Tennessee appointed Dr. John L. Paz to the State Child Abuse and Neglect Prevention Board.

- He was a member of the Christian Childcare Association. He was a former president of the Southern Association of Childcare Workers. He was a board member of the Christian Child and Family Services Association.

- John was a marriage counselor. He was compassionate and understanding and helped many people in their troubled lives.

- He and his wife are the parents of a daughter and son who are both teachers and did missionary work themselves.

- Dr. John L. Paz is well loved and respected in the community and around many parts of the world.

Some of this is repetition, but this is a condensed form of John's activities throughout his life. These are just a few of the extraordinary accomplishments that happened because of the pain and agony of John's subconscious negative core beliefs, which spurred him with great drive and energy to pursue with his whole being, to overcompensate, so he would not go to hell. Because he suffered from this unhealthy belief and other negative core beliefs, the Brazilians, Albanians, Russians, and Americans all benefited so much, as he touched many people on three continents of the world, which produced intense energy that resulted in so many accomplishments.

History of John L. Paz's Breakdown Beginning in 2002

his is the chronologic order that condenses the events, if the reader is interested.

On August 2002, John suddenly manifested severe obsessive/compulsive behavior; he was on a high and slept only two or three hours a night. He worked day and night.

On November 2002, I asked his family physician to give John lithium, as I could tell he was on an agitated manic high. John started seeing Dr. Smith, a psychiatrist, around January 2003. Dr. Smith changed his medication to Lexapro, along with Depakote instead of lithium.

On February 25, 2003, John was in such a deep, debilitating depression that I had to check him into the emergency room at St. Mary's Psych Geriatric Unit in Memphis, Tennessee.

He had no taste and no hunger for almost five months and lost about fifty pounds. He also lost his sense of smell. At one time, he actually had three psychiatrists. John was released from the hospital in March 2003.

John's mental state deteriorated, and so on July 11, 2004, I put him back in the hospital on the psychiatric ward in Memphis for the second time. He stayed for two weeks. The doctor discharged him because I agreed to take him to stay with his mother and sisters, who lived in Kentucky. He could be taken care of twenty-four hours a day if he stayed with them, as I had to work during the day. He still continued to struggle. The medicines didn't seem to help, and there were side effects to some of the drugs.

On July 24, 2004, the board of directors met and accepted John's resignation as director of Wilson Children's Home. On Thursday, July 29, 2004, I took John to stay with his mother and sisters in Lexington, Kentucky. He needed to spend a long time getting well there.

On August 11, John was suffering from retention of the urinary tract, due to the serious side effect of taking Abilify. He was taken to the emergency room in Lexington. He had to get off Abilify fast.

John went to the new psychiatrist, Dr. Wright, at the Bailey Psychiatric Center in Lexington on August 30, 2004. He changed John's medicine. He put him back on lithium and a new medicine and took him off Zoloft, Abilify, and Depakote.

John did not improve at all during those two weeks following this formula. While John was in Kentucky, he got word that his wonderful psychiatrist of a year and a half in Memphis had put a gun to his head and killed himself. John really liked that doctor, and so it was another great loss for him.

Early in 2005, John had a new psychiatrist, Dr. Higgins. He saw him only a few times. Dr. Higgins did tell me that most likely, John was on a mild high, or hypomania, for most of his life. Dr. Jackie Robinson replaced Dr. Higgins, and she really respected John and tried to help his depressive condition. It is interesting to note that Dr. Robinson's mother many years ago was a secretary at Wilson Children's Home, where John had been the executive director. She put John on Wellbutrin and increased his Lexapro, along with another drug for anxiety. It helped some with his anxiety. Later, Dr.

Robinson took John off Lexapro and put him on Cymbalta. He had an MRI due to the fact that he had enlarged glands on top of his eyes, and it was a cause of concern, as it could have been cancerous. The MRI showed that the glands were enlarged, but it was not cancer. There was no abnormality in his brain, so he just suffers deep depression and anxiety due to bipolar disorder.

March 9, 2006: John met with Dr. Robinson, and this time she added Ritalin to get him started in the morning; however, he could not take that as it made him extremely nervous. Dr. Robinson referred John to Dr. Clary in Nashville, Tennessee, to be a candidate for the vagus nerve stimulator implant (VNS). This implant has had great success for many people with conquering treatment–resistant depression (TRD)

On April 28, 2006, John and I arrived at St. Francis Hospital at 4:30 a.m., and he had surgery at 7:59 a.m. The surgery normally takes one to two hours but it only took forty minutes, and all went well. John awoke from the operation in a good mood, talking with some friends. In the next several days, I noticed a positive change in John. His mood was elevated, and he spent less time in bed. However, he did suffer one day of a setback, but the next day he was feeling better. His wounds healed fast. The only side effect was that he had hoarseness in his voice, and that is the most common side effect. John kept on improving. His low times didn't seem to last as long as they used to. He started laughing two weeks after his surgery. He joked with someone and showed other little positive changes that were so encouraging. This improvement did not last long.

John, our daughter, Mary, and I took a vacation in June 2006. We went to nine states; Niagara Falls, Canada; Washington, DC; the beaches of North and South Carolina; and through the Smoky and the Appalachian Mountains—over 3,400 miles. John enjoyed every day immensely, but when we got close to home, he fell into a depression. The doctor continued to increase the intensity of the implant to where it should be to stimulate the brain to produce those necessary neurotransmitters. The doctor had a magnetic hand control that she put over John's implant, and this enabled her to raise the vibration higher in the hope that would relieve John's depression. The doctors warned that it might take six months to a year to fully achieve the desired results of mood elevation; unfortunately, it never helped him for more than a few days.

About a year after John had the implant, a hearing came up with Medicare, evaluating this procedure to see if they would continue to pay for this device. Hundreds of doctors, patients, relatives, and others posted letters on the Internet, urging Medicare and insurance companies to fund this implant, as it has helped so many people with this debilitating condition. The cost was thirty thousand dollars. Medicare and our insurance paid most of the cost. This truly can transform a person with TRD. Unfortunately, early in February 2007, the Centers for Medicare & Medicaid Services (CMS) issued its proposed decision to deny payment for the vagus nerve stimulator, which truly is a breakthrough treatment for sufferers of chronic or treatment-resistant depression. This implant is still approved by the FDA. For more information, the web site is www.vagusnervestimulation.com.

After ten months of John's having the implant, I was frustrated that he had not made as many great strides in his recovery as I thought would occur. He was improving slowly, but my expectations were high, so on February 8, 2007, I e-mailed the author of the only book on the market at that time regarding the implant and told him of my frustration. Within fifteen minutes, he sent me an e-mail, informing me that many people do not respond that dramatically until after a year of implantation and that I should be patient because, as he put it, "Your husband's brain is being rewired, and that takes time." The doctor told me that I would notice small improvements in his behavior, and I definitely saw that at first.

This mental picture of John's mind being rewired helped me to have more patience in what was going on in his brain. This was all so exciting and new, as I realized that John depleted so much of his neurotransmitters and that now this implant was shooting electrical impulses through the vagus nerve to his brain to replenish the serotonin and epinephrine. This VNS originally was given to epileptics, and the doctors also noticed such measurable mood elevations in these patients. That is why this method was used on resistant depressive patients.

On March 15, 2007, John's psychiatrist took him off Wellbutrin. He had been taking it for two years. We wanted to see if Wellbutrin was really helping him or, as in rare cases, antidepressants can actually make depression worse. As it turned out, John went downhill fast, and so we realized that he indeed needed this antidepressant. He started back on Wellbutrin, and there was a dramatic change. However, John still had his good days and bad days, so he was still struggling. Incredibly, in April 2007, John had nine good days in a row. This was a record and the first time in four years of deep depression that he sustained so many days free of depression. Was the vagus nerve implant now kicking in? In May 2007, John talked to the new director of Wilson Children's Home about doing volunteer work for the children's home. He sat in on intake cases and offered his opinion to the caseworkers on whether they should admit a child to the home. There were some applicants that would not be appropriate for Wilson Children's Home's program, such as those who were suicidal, dangerous to others, or sexual perverts. John also visited shut-ins, but he was still suffering from anxiety and depression.

In June 2007, John and I went to visit our daughter in Oklahoma City, who taught English as a second language to children from all over the world. John seemed to enjoy the visit and was doing well, but when we got close to home, he fell back into a depression. Our home represents failure, bad memories, and agony from his mental breakdown. Then, a few weeks later, we went to a family reunion in Indiana. I believed that John could work through this condition.

On July 2008, John's psychiatrist added the antidepressant he used to take, Cymbalta. However, John had a severe drug reaction and had to stop taking it after four days. Then one month later in August, the doctor gave John the new antidepressant, Luvox. John also had a drug reaction again and stopped taking it. Along with the Luvox, John was given the anti-anxiety drug, Ativan, but at this point his nerves were shot, and so he stopped that medicine. He struggled with shaking and terrible nervousness. I suspected that John may have had Parkinson's disease, but after much research I decided he did not have this disease. The shaking was caused by the medicines he was taking.

In January 2009, John started seeing a new therapist. He had a favorable opinion of her, but he seemed to be deteriorating as he had to spend more and more time in bed.

On May 2, 2009, I noticed a difference in John, and a week later, on Friday, May 8, I came home at noon, expecting to find John in bed in a deep depression, but instead he was in the dining room at the table with his Bible and reference books, writing several pages of Bible lesson plans. Because of his nervousness, he had not been able to write for the previous six years of his mental illness, as his hands shook so badly. That day, his writing was just the way he used to write before his illness. This was incredible! He had not been able to concentrate on any project like this, so I knew something in his brain was changing for the good.

The next day, however, he had a setback. He drove to the gym and on the way back, he backed into another car. He was terribly upset—this was the second time within a few weeks that he had backed into someone's car. It shook him up, and I was afraid it would really set him back. The next day, he did all right but was noticeably nervous and badly shaken by the event. John was extremely fragile, mentally. I had to take his car keys away from him, and that was another loss in his life.

In July 2009, his psychiatrist gave him another medicine, Remeron. After a few days, he showed some signs of feeling better, but that didn't last long.

On December 22, 2009, we moved from Memphis to our new home in Oklahoma City, Oklahoma. Our daughter had built a beautiful new home with five bedrooms, and we moved in with her. In February, John met with a psychotherapist in Oklahoma City. This therapist was very insightful, but he was too expensive for us. I believe he was able to get the closest to John's inscrutable mind and the agony that was in his heart. Then on March 4, 2010, John had his first appointment with a new psychiatrist in Oklahoma City. The doctor couldn't believe John had taken all those medicines over the past seven years. He recognized all the side effects. So the doctor took him gradually off risperidone and the generic form of Wellbutrin. On that date, he started taking Artane for his tremors. It had been four years since he was implanted with the vagus nerve implant, but John did not benefit from this procedure. John suffered with anxiety attacks for many months. On April 30, 2010, his psychotherapist showed him a way he could counter this terror that he felt inside. He asked John where it hurt and said to put his arms around his waist, starting from the lower stomach and going up, stopping where his pain was. John took his hands at his lower stomach and stopped at his heart. The therapist asked what color it was, and John immediately said red and described the shape and how wide it was. Then the therapist told John that when he got these anxiety attacks, he should slowly hold that pain with a lot of kindness and love. He explained that quite often, people get hurt some way when they are very young, and it goes into the brain as amnesia. Then, at some point much later in life, during extreme stress, it comes out and causes a lot of pain and terror. John kept saying he didn't know what he was afraid of, and we were so frustrated when he had these attacks. The source of his problems lodged deep in his subconscious mind from negative cellular memories and false beliefs. He kept saying that he hurt in his heart.

On May 25, 2010, Dr. Mendoza gave John a drug that he had never taken—Tegretol, a mood stabilizer. After twenty-four hours of taking this medicine, it completely relieved him of all the nervousness and anxiety. This was amazing, and he kept on saying he felt better. After all the medicines, shock treatments, hospital stays, the VNS implant, it was this one medicine that cured him! However, after about five days John said that the medicine was wearing off. He fell again into the depths of depression, nervousness, and anxiety. He made statements like, "I feel like I am dying inside," and "When I go to bed tonight, I don't want to wake up." I believe these expressions were the beginning of suicidal thoughts. His eyes and facial expressions showed so much torment and agony. I felt so frustrated because I did not know what would give him relief. At that point, I wondered if he had brain damage, a chemical imbalance, or something else. Nothing seemed to work.

John stopped seeing this psychotherapist at the end of May 2010. On June 13, 2010, he started therapy with a new therapist. I was very impressed with this therapist, as he used cognitive therapy, which I think could have helped John. He believed John overcompensated all his life, excelling in so many areas because of the wrong core belief that he was going to hell. He believed a lie; this led to behavior where he tried to prove his self-worth, and he would do anything to show God that he shouldn't be damned eternally.

John's Medicines from 2002 to 2012

1. Lithium   –   mood stabilizer
2. Trazadone   –   antidepressant
3. Lexapro   –   antidepressant (only took it for about a week)
4. Depakote   –   mood stabilizer
5. Prozac   –   antidepressant
6. Inderal   –   beta blocker for tremors
7. Seroquel   –   antipsychotic
8. Risperidone   –   antipsychotic
9. Lamictal   –   mood stabilizer
10. Zoloft   –   antidepressant
11. Lorezepam   –   anti-anxiety
12. Ambien   –   sleeping pills
13. Xanax   –   anti-anxiety
14. Abilify   –   antipsychotic (serious side affect for John)
15. Wellbutrin   –   antidepressant
16. Klonopin   –   anti-anxiety
17. Cymbalta   –   antidepressant
18. Ritalin   –   stimulant
19. Luvox   –   had a reaction to this
20. Tegretol   –   mood stabilizer
21. Zyprexa   –   antipsychotic
22. Propranolol   –   high blood pressure
23. Norvasc   –   high blood pressure

24. Buspar   –   for bipolar
25. Gabapentin   –   for bipolar; (terrible invasive thoughts)
26. Remeron   –   antidepressant
27. Viibryd   –   antidepressant

Psychiatrists Who Treated John

1. Dr. Richard Smith—only for a couple of months prior to entering the hospital.
2. Dr. Tim Barnes only treated John in the hospital those sixteen days.
3. Dr. Bill Green was his doctor from February 2003 to 2004.
4. Dr. Carl Peterson gave him two ECT treatments.
5. Dr. Lynn Davis gave him seven ECT treatments.
6. Dr. George Adams treated him for two weeks in the hospital.
7. Dr. Leonard Wright treated John during his stay in Kentucky with family.
8. Dr. Ralph Higgins saw him two times and then resigned.
9. Dr. Jackie Robinson treated John in mid-2005 to December 2009.
10. Dr. Juan Mendoza—from March 2010 to September 2010.
11. Dr. Angelo D. Christian—from September 25, 2010, to September 8, 2011.
12. Dr. John Williams—from November 2011 to present.

Hospitals Where John Was Treated

1. St. Mary's Geriatric Psych Unit, Memphis, Tennessee, sixteen days in February 2003.
2. Carter Hospital, Memphis, where he had nine electric shock treatments (ECT) and spent one night.
3. St. Mary's Geriatric Psych Unit, Memphis. He stayed fourteen days again in July 2004.
4. St. Thomas ER in Memphis, 2010.
5. Baptist Medical Center, Memphis (one night).
6. Cedar Adventist Hospital, Nashville, Tennessee, for six weeks, from September to November 2010.

Glossary

1. **Alpha brain wave**—alpha is where you are relaxed and can focus and meditate.
2. **Awareness**—the state of being conscious, perceiving, knowing and understanding.
3. **Beta brain wave**—this includes a deeper concentration, arousal, and alertness.
4. **Biomagnetic**—where the tissue and organs in the body produce specific magnetic vibration. They call them biomagnetic fields.
5. **Bipolar disorder**—a mental disorder where a person goes into a manic state or a depressive state of mind, and some people experience both manic and depressive.
6. **Brain synchronization**—the connection of the right and left brains.
7. **Brain wave therapy**—the method of listening to mind-enhancing CDs can process our thoughts through this technology and synchronize the two brains.
8. **Brain-Wave Entrainment**—a fairly new technology, where these CDs cause brain waves to help synchronize the left and right brains.
9. **Cellular memories**—feelings and actions that can be attributed to unconscious memories stored in our bodies. Southwestern Medical School calls them cellular memories.

10. **Cognitive behavior**—to notice, recognize, or to be aware and conscious.

11. **Conscious mind**—a state of being aware. Reasoning and logic are in the conscious mind.

12. **Core beliefs**—our innermost negative or positive beliefs that we acquire throughout life, especially as children.

13. **Delta brain wave**—the deepest brain wave, a dreamless sleep.

14. **Depression**—profound sadness and despondency and very negative; without joy.

15. **Emotion Code**—uses muscle testing to release trapped emotions for abundant health, love, and happiness.

16. **Empowerment**—to permit or enable someone to accomplish goals, once the person is freed of self-limiting and self-sabotaging behavior.

17. **Energy frequency**—everything at its root is an energy frequency ($E=mc^2$), and that illness and disease can be traced to an unhealthy energy frequency.

18. **Enlightenment**—to illuminate and make aware, as enlighten the eyes of your heart.

19. **Genius Code**—a program pointing out that we are brighter, sharper, and smarter than we think.

20. **Healing Codes**—a method that can change the negative beliefs into a positive state of mind.

21. **Holosync audio technology**—creates the brain wave patterns of meditation, along with many other beneficial states, instant mental abilities; has been used by well over one million people in 193 countries.

22. **Hypothalamus**—an area of the brain that produces hormones that control body temperature, hunger, moods.

23. **Image streaming**—condition your own mind through a simple process, where you tap into the unending flow of images and thoughts that flow from your mind.

24. **Inspiration**—creative thought; inspiration comes from the right brain.

25. **Intuitive**—innate, natural, inborn, extrasensory perception, telepathic, psychic, informal hunch, insight; also resides in the right brain.

26. **Left brain**—contains the logical and analytical processing.

27. **Manifestation**—to exhibit, reveal, evidence, expression.

28. **Mental health**—a state of the mind, being rational.

29. **Muscle testing**—communicating with the subconscious mind, much like a lie detector shows whether a person is telling the truth. We have a physical response when we tell the truth or tell a lie. The muscles are instantly weakened when we lie. They stay strong when we tell the truth.

30. **Neuro-cognitive scientist**—studies perception in the brain.

31. **Neuro-pathways**—pathways that communicate between the right and left brain hemispheres.

32. **Neurological heritage**—vast abilities that can be used to improve the quality of life for you, your family, friends, and community.

33. **Paraliminal**—*para* is from the Greek meaning "beyond," and *liminal* is Greek meaning "threshold," which together mean "beyond the threshold of conscious awareness."

34. **Potentiality**—ability, possible, conceivable.

35. **Qi**—Chinese energy field.

36. **Quantum physics**—a branch of science that deals with discrete, indivisible units of energy called quanta, as described by the quantum theory. It describes the nature of the universe as being

much different from the world we see. Another definition: the study of the behavior of matter and energy at the molecular, atomic, nuclear, subatomic and even smaller microscopic levels.

37. **Right brain**—the right brain contains the creativity, inspiration, and intuitive abilities.

38. **Subconscious mind**—the subconscious mind holds the emotions that fuel and drive our conscious thinking. The subconscious mind controls insight and wisdom. It is our connection to a higher authority—God.

39. **Theta brain wave**—the pattern of increased creativity, visionary experiences and a deeper meditation.

40. **Transmutation**—the changing or transferring of one element or form of energy into another, as in sexual transmutation, channeling this energy into creativity and spirituality.

41. **Vibration and vibration energy**—conscious frequency of love; all the organs in the body produce specific magnetic vibration; everything that exists radiates vibrational energy. The higher the vibration, the better life is for an individual; qualities such as love, gratitude, joy, peace and the rest of the fruits of the Spirit are manifested.

42. **Whole-brain thinking**—altered brain-wave patterns using both left and right brain sides simultaneously.

Suggested Resources

Ronald R. Fieve, MD, *Moodswing: The Third Revolution in Psychiatry* (New York: Bantam Books, 1975, and reprinted).

Bill Harris, *Thresholds of the Mind, Your Personal Roadmap to Success, Happiness, and Contentment* (Beaverton, OR: Centerpointe Press, 2007).

Napoleon Hill, *Think and Grow Rich: The Original 1937 Version* (The Ralston Society, 1937). Published and distributed by www. asamanthinketh.net. No Dream Too Big, LLC, PO Box 1220, Melrose, FL 32666.

Richard Gordon, *Quantum-Touch, The Power to Heal* (Berkeley: North Atlantic Books, 2006).

John A. Scott Sr., *Hypnoanalysis for Individual and Marital Psychotherapy* (New York: NY Gardner Press, Inc., 1993).

Joseph Henry Thayer in *A Greek English Lexicon of the New Testament.* Corrected Edition (New York: American Book, 1989), 643.

Jan Wiener, *The Therapeutic Relationship: Transference, Countertransference, and the Making of Meaning.* Fay Series in Analytical Psychology (Book 14). (College Station, TX: Texas A & M, 2009).

Websites and Webinars

Robert Anthony, "Manifestation Intelligence," www.drrobertanthony.com

Richard Bandler and John Grinder, "thoughtsinspire.com

Craig Beck, "The Now Method," www.thenowmethod.com

Alan B. Densky, www.neuro-vision.us

Bill Harris, www.centerpointe.com

Ben Johnson and Alexander Loyd, www.thehealingcodes.com

Kenji Kumara, www.newtransformationstrategies.com

Paul Scheele and Win Wenger, www.learningstrategies.com and

www.learningstrategies.com/geniuscode

Christie Marie Sheldon, "Love or Above," www.loveorabove.com

CPSIA information can be obtained at www.ICGtesting.com
Printed in the USA
BVOW071955210413

318644BV00003B/7/P

9 781449 790097